FUTURE SCENARIOS

How Communities
Can Adapt to Peak Oil
and Climate Change

DAVID HOLMGREN

First published in the UK in 2009
by Green Books
Foxhole, Dartington, Totnes,
Devon TQ9 6EB
www.greenbooks.co.uk

Based on the US edition published by
Chelsea Green Publishing Company,
White River Junction, Vermont

Project Manager: Emily Foote
Editor: Cannon Labrie
Proofreader: Helen Walden
Designer: Peter Holm,
Sterling Hill Productions

Printed in the UK by Latimer Trend, Plympton, Devon, UK
on 100% recycled paper.

ISBN 978 1 900322 50 8

CONTENTS

ACKNOWLEDGEMENTS

This book has its origins, and continuing life, as a website (futurescenarios.org) that is my contribution to stimulating awareness and positive responses to peak oil and climate change by community and environmental activists. My introduction to scenario planning dates from my frequent, long and varied discussions with friend and change-management consultant Steve Bright during the late 1990s. My first use of scenario planning to integrate peak oil and climate change was in a presentation to government officials and environmental activists in Adelaide, focused on updating the South Australian government's State Strategy Plan. That presentation was part of my Peak Oil and Permaculture tour of Australian capital cities with Richard Heinberg in 2006. Close contact and discussions with Heinberg, along with his books, most notably *Powerdown*, influenced my thinking about the scenarios.

Websites and discussion forums on the Internet related to peak oil, energy, climate change and permaculture have also been a major source of information and ideas, in particular Energy Bulletin (energybulletin.net) and The Oil Drum (theoildrum.com). Adam Grubb, founding editor of Energy Bulletin, has had a unique role in this project. In 2004 he interviewed me about peak oil, permaculture and the future of the suburbs. The following year he attended a two-week permaculture design course that I co-taught in Bendigo, central Victoria. Since then Adam has played a pivotal role in the spread of awareness, through peak-oil networks, of permaculture as a grassroots response to energy descent. In 2006 he published a brief article I wrote about the scenarios on Energy

Bulletin and encouraged me to write a more in-depth essay. After further development and workshopping of the scenarios in advanced permaculture courses in New Zealand and Latin America in 2007, Adam suggested and collabourated in publishing a website version of this essay. He used his considerable web skills and connections to co-create and publish the website in May 2008. In publishing on the Web we were aiming to get the ideas out as quickly as possibly.

The proposal for this book came from Margo Baldwin at Chelsea Green. Margo recognised the potential for its publication as a traditional book to complement other books published and distributed by Chelsea Green about permaculture and related approaches for responding to the energy/climate crisis. One such book is *The Transition Handbook* by British permaculture activist Rob Hopkins, who has spread awareness of the energy-descent concept and proactive responses that households and communities can make to adapt creatively to energy descent in the face of denial and obfuscation by governments. As a result, the viral spread of transition activism has provided a strong affirmation that permaculture thinking can be a powerful catalyst for creative community-based responses to energy descent. Beyond the great achievers of permaculture activism such as Rob Hopkins, I am incredibly indebted, as one of the co-originators of the permaculture concept, to the countless others who have used permaculture to help change their own lives and, in the process, have helped to increase the credibility of permaculture as a force for positive change. This book is an attempt to help those already along the path pioneered by permaculture and related movements to recognise the storms and the opportunities of the peak-oil and climate-change era. If it manages to contribute to slightly less dysfunctional public-policy decisions as we move deeper into the global crisis, then that will be a bonus.

Finally I would like to acknowledge my parents for raising me to struggle to understand the big picture, question authority, and work for a more equitable world.

Hepburn, Victoria, Australia
August 2008

INTRODUCTION: ENERGY AND HISTORY

THE SIMULTANEOUS ONSET of climate change and the peaking of global oil supply represent unprecedented challenges for human civilisation.

Global oil peak has the potential to shake or even destroy the foundations of global industrial economy and culture. Climate change has the potential to rearrange the biosphere more radically than the last ice age. Each limits the effective options for responses to the other.

The strategies for mitigating the adverse effects and/or adapting to the consequences of climate change have mostly been considered and discussed in isolation from those relevant to peak oil. While awareness of peak oil, or at least energy crisis, is increasing, understanding of how the two problems of climate change and peak oil might interact to generate quite different futures is still at an early stage.

Over the last thirty-five years the climate-damaging impacts of fossil-fuel burning and other sources of 'greenhouse gases' has shifted from being a worrying hypothesis of some climate scientists to one of the primary drivers of environmental awareness, from the schoolroom to the boardroom. Rapid economic growth in developing economies, especially China and India, addictive consumer economies in the long-affluent West, and ongoing population growth are driving emissions ever higher. Meanwhile the evidence of actual climate change is accelerating, with the alarming rates of Arctic sea ice melting being the most dramatic. This is belatedly creating an urgency in the halls of government and international legal conventions. Economic policy in the affluent countries is gradually shifting under the weight of evidence that economies must be decarbonised whether or not that reduces economic growth.

During the twentieth century, most thinking about the future was based on the assumption that technological and organisational complexity will continually expand in lockstep with economic growth. The most substantial challenge to those assumptions about the future was the modelling work of Jay Forrester and colleagues in the *Limits to Growth Report* (1972) commissioned by the Club of Rome, a prestigious international public policy 'think tank'.

While the energy crises of the 1970s illustrated the vulnerability of industrial society to oil shortage, the oil glut and low prices of the 1980s, combined with a barrage of misinformation, saw these ideas lose favour. A whole generation of economists, politicians, businesspeople and even environmentalists learned that, for better or worse, the limits of resources were not going to threaten 'business as usual'.

It is only the recent escalation of energy and commodity prices that has seen energy, resources and the limits of nature again being widely recognised as the key drivers in human economic systems. This return to notions of limits so clearly outlined 36 years ago has also raised the spectre of the more fundamental scarcity of food, identified more than 150 years earlier by Thomas Malthus. Rising food prices are now widely recognised as being driven directly and indirectly by the cost of energy. The demand for biofuel, the cost of energy-dense fertilisers, climate-change-related droughts, water scarcity, and the impact of rising affluence driving increases in meat consumption from agribusiness-production systems are all contributing to this global crisis. Those who suggest the likely return of the four horsemen of the apocalypse (famine,

Figure 1. A Cuban sunset silhouetting powerlines and an oil-fired power-station smokestack. Cuba is still recovering from the fuel and electricity shortages that crippled the economy and food supply in the 1990s. The Cuban experience is emblematic of the current global energy crisis. Photo by Oliver Holmgren.

pestilence, war and death) are more vocal than ever before despite being labeled Malthusian or just 'doomer'.

The evidence that global industrial civilisation is in the early stage of an energy transition as fundamental as the one from renewable resources to fossil fuels is overwhelming. Using the ecological history of past civilisations as a base, I review the evidence about the future in terms of four possible long-term scenarios: *techno-explosion*, *techno-stability*, *energy descent* and *collapse*. While faith in techno-explosion as the default scenario is now waning, the hope of more environmentally aware citizens and organisations depends on techno-stability, characterised by novel renewable energy sources, while the fears of total collapse of human civilisation are continually fed by evidence about climate change and resource depletion, among a range of related emerging crises. Energy descent, where available energy and resulting organisational complexity progressively decline over many generations, is the most ignored of the four possible long-term futures, but I think the evidence is strong and increasing that it is the most likely in some form or other.

Rather than gathering together all of the evidence to support the claim for the energy-descent future, I build on thirty years of permaculture thinking and activism to further develop the thinking tools that can help us all adapt to energy descent as it unfolds, irrespective of whether we believe it to be humanity's fate. Energy descent is likely to give birth to a new culture, one more different from our current globalised culture than post-Enlightenment capitalism and industrial culture was from its precursors in Europe. The energetic contraction will force a relocalisation of economies, simplified technology, a ruralisation of populations away from very large cities, and a reduction in total population. Over time there will be a redevelopment of localised cultures and even new languages, although these developments may be outside the time frame of the peak-oil and climate-change scenarios described here. I focus on four plausible scenarios by which peak oil and climate change could generate the early stages, over the next ten to thirty years, of the energy-descent future.

Permaculture is a design system for sustainable land use and living that was proposed by Bill Mollison and me during the 1970s, when the evidence for the energy-descent future was growing strongly. Exploitation of new oil and natural gas resources in the 1980s and 1990s allowed resurgent economic growth. In the process our hopes for a graceful energy descent supported by ecological design, appropriate technology and relocalised economies were dashed. Nevertheless, permaculture has spread around the world. This spread has reflected both mounting disaffection with consumer culture in affluent countries and the increasingly desperate needs of those left behind by development in poor countries. As energy and food costs now rise around the world and disaffection worsens with the inability of governments to deal with the emerging energy and environmental crisis, permaculture is attracting increased attention from those acting to secure their families' future and contribute to a better world. As a conceptual framework, a collection of practical strategies and a self-help and grassroots movement, permaculture provides the hope and the tools to allow humanity to weather the storms and even thrive in a world of progressively less and less available energy. The energy-descent concept was an explicit foundation for my articulation and explanation of permaculture concepts in *Permaculture: Principles and Pathways Beyond Sustainability*, published in 2002, just before the current rapid rise in oil and commodity prices began to stimulate wider interest in energy descent. This new book uses permaculture thinking to tell stories about the energy-descent future that can empower us to take adaptive and positive action.

ENERGETIC AND ECOLOGICAL FOUNDATIONS OF HUMAN HISTORY

The broad processes of human history can be understood using an ecological framework that recognises primary energy sources as the strongest factors determining the general structure of human economy, politics and culture. The transition from a hunter-gatherer way of life to that of settled agriculture made possible the expansion of human numbers, denser settlement patterns and surplus resources. Those surplus resources were the foundations for what we call civilisation, including the development of more advanced technologies, cities, social class structures, standing armies and written language. Archaeology records a series of civilisations that rose and fell as they depleted their bioregional resource base.

Lower-density simple agrarian and hunter-gatherer cultures took over the territory of collapsed civilisations and allowed the resources of forests, soils and water to regenerate. That, in turn, gave rise to new cycles of growth in cultural complexity.

In the European Renaissance, the medieval systems that evolved from the remnants of the Roman Empire were reinfused with knowledge and culture from the Islamic and Asian civilisations and grew into competing nation-states. A combination of the demands of internal growth and warfare between nations almost exhausted the carrying capacity of Europe. As this ecological crisis deepened in the fourteenth and fifteenth centuries, European exploration in search of new resources carried the 'diseases of crowding' around the world. In the Americas, up to 90 per cent of many populations died, leaving vast resources to plunder. Starting with the plundering of precious metals and seeds of valuable crop plants such as corn and potatoes, European nations soon moved on to building empires powered by slavery that allowed them to exploit and colonise the new lands well stocked with timber, animals and fertile soils, all rejuvenating in the wake of the collapse of indigenous populations.

European population, culture (especially capitalism), and technology then grew strong enough to tap vast stocks of novel energy that were useless to previous simpler societies.

European coal fuelled the Industrial Revolution while food and other basic commodities from colonies helped solve the limits to food production in Europe. As industrialisation spread in North America and later in Russia, oil quickly surpassed coal as the most valuable energy source, and accelerated the jump in human population from one billion in 1800 to two billion in 1930 to now over six billion in one lifetime. This massive growth in human carrying capacity has been made possible by the consumption of vast stocks of nonrenewable resources (in addition to expanding demand on the renewable

> The history of the twentieth century makes more sense when interpreted primarily as the struggle for control of oil rather than the clash of ideologies.

biological resources of the planet). Rapid rates of urbanisation and migration, technology change, increasing affluence and disparity of wealth, as well as unprecedented conflicts between global and regional powers, have accompanied this transition.

The history of the twentieth century makes more sense when interpreted primarily as the struggle for control of oil rather than the clash of ideologies.[1] In emphasising the primacy of energy resources I am not saying that the great struggles between ideologies, especially capitalism and socialism, have not been important in shaping history, but most teaching and understanding of history underestimates the importance of energetic, ecological and economic factors.

The fact that conflict has increased as available resources have expanded is hard to explain using conventional thinking. One way to understand this is using older moral concepts about more power leading to greater moral degradation. Another equally useful way to understand this is using ecological thinking. When resources are minimal and diffuse, energy spent by one human group, tribe or nation to capture those resources can be greater than what is gained. As resources become more concentrated (by grain agriculture, for example, and even more dramatically by tapping fossil fuels), the resources captured through diplomacy, trade and even war are often much greater than the effort expended.

The final phase in the fossil-fuel saga is playing out now, as the transition from oil to natural gas and lower-quality oil resources accelerates, with massive new infrastructure developments around the world as well as increasing tension and

> The final phase in the fossil-fuel saga is playing out now, as the transition from oil to natural gas and lower-quality oil resources accelerates.

active conflicts over resources. We can only hope that nations and humanity as a whole learn quickly that using resources to capture resources will yield less return and incur escalating costs and risks in a world of depleting and diffuse energy.

THE NEXT ENERGY TRANSITION

Quite early in the exploitation of fossil resources, the debate began about what happens after their exhaustion, but it has remained mostly academic. The post-World-War-II period of sustained growth, affluence and freedom from the adverse effects of war had the effect of entrenching the faith in human power and the inexorable arrow of progress that would lead to more of whatever we desired.[2] Consideration of external limits or cultural constraints on affluence remained at the fringe. Throughout most of the twentieth century, a range of energy sources (from nuclear to solar) have been proposed as providing the next 'free' energy source that will replace fossil fuels.[3]

In so-called developing countries, the power of the dominant globalist culture, both as a model to emulate and a mode of exploitation to resist, preoccupied most thinkers, leaders and activists. The key issue was how to get a share of the pie, not the limits to the size of the pie.

But the super-accelerated growth in energy per person of the post-World-War-II era came to an end with the energy crisis of 1973, when OPEC countries moved to exert their power through oil supply and price. The publication of the seminal *Limits to Growth* report in 1972 had defined the problem and the consequences by modelling how a range of limits would constrain industrial society in the early twenty-first century. After the second oil shock in 1979 the debate about the next energy transition intensified, but by 1983 a series of factors pushed energy supply off the agenda. Economic contraction, not seen since the US Depression of the 1930s, had reduced demand and consequently prices for energy and natural resources. In affluent countries, the conversion from oil to gas and nuclear for electricity generation reduced demand for oil. Energy-efficiency gains in vehicles and industry further reduced demand. Most importantly, the new supergiant oilfields in the North Sea and Alaska reduced Western dependence on OPEC and depressed the price even further. All other primary commodity prices followed the downward trend set by oil because cheap energy could be used to substitute for other needed commodities.[4]

The economies of the affluent countries were further boosted by two important changes. The shift from Keynesian to Friedmanite free-market economic policies reduced regulatory impediments to business and enlisted public wealth for new private profits. At the same time, the debt crisis in developing countries triggered by collapsing commodity prices didn't slow the flow of interest repayments into the coffers of Western banks. In line with the new free-market ideology, structural adjustment packages from the International Monetary Fund and World Bank provided more loans (and debt) on the condition that developing countries slash education, health and other public services to conserve funds for repayments.

The scientific consensus about global warming in the late 1980s and early 1990s renewed the focus on reducing fossil fuel use, not to conserve resources, which were widely thought to be abundant, but to reduce carbon dioxide additions to the atmosphere. But with energy prices low owing to a glut of oil, the main action was an acceleration in the shift to gas as a cheap and relatively 'clean' fuel.

Half a century earlier, in 1956, the startling predictions by eminent petroleum geologist M. King Hubbert that oil production in the United States, the world's largest producer, would peak in 1970, had almost destroyed Hubbert's career and reputation. Ironically, the controversy within the oil industry over Hubbert's methodology and predictions was not known by the authors of the *Limits to Growth* report and was not part of the 1970s public debate over limits of resources. It was nearly a decade later, at the depth of the greatest economic recession since the 1930s, that the industry acknowledged that oil production in the lower forty-eight states had in fact peaked and declined, despite the greatest drilling programme in history. Hubbert also estimated a global oil peak early in the twenty-first century.

Figure 2. Freeway in Raleigh, North Carolina, at rush hour, 2005: the classic symbol of automobile dependence in the United States, where private cars and light trucks used mostly for personal mobility account for about 43 per cent of total oil consumption.

In the mid 1990s the work of independent and retired petroleum geologists who were colleagues of Hubbert reviewed his original predictions using new information and evidence, triggering the debate about peak oil that grew and spread along with the Internet in the last years of the millennium. But with the cost of oil as low as ten dollars a barrel, the gurus of economics and oil supply quoted in the mainstream media thought that oil was on the way to becoming worthless and redundant through glut and technological advances. The delusions of cheap energy were widespread. Ironically, many environmentalists concerned about the mounting evidence of, and inaction of governments about, climate change, put their faith in the 'hydrogen economy' powered by clean renewable technologies to save us from polluting the planet to death.

While energy and consequently food costs in affluent countries remained the lowest in human history, the evidence for energy descent rather than ascent made little impact outside the counterculture. Since 2004 the rising cost of energy, and now food, is focusing the attention of leaders and the masses on questions of sustainability not seen since the energy crises of the 1970s.

The research, activism and awareness of energy and climate issues provide a context for the growing debate about the ecological, economic and social sustainability of everything from agriculture to human-settlement patterns and even fundamental human values and beliefs. There is a huge body of evidence that the next energy transition will not follow the pattern of recent centuries to more concentrated and powerful sources.

The likelihood that this transition will be to one of less energy is so anathema to the psychosocial foundations and power elites of modern societies that it is constantly misinterpreted, ignored, covered up or derided. Instead we see geopolitical manoeuvring around energy resources, including proxy and real wars to control dwindling reserves and policy gymnastics to somehow make reducing carbon emissions the new engine of economic growth.

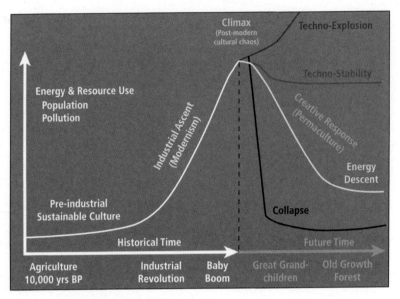

Figure 3. Four energy futures.

Techno-stability depends on a seamless conversion from material growth based on depleting energy to a steady state in consumption of resources and population (if not economic activity), all based on novel use of renewable energies and technologies that can maintain if not improve the quality of services available from current systems. While this clearly involves massive change in almost all aspects of society, the implication is that once sustainable systems are set in place, a steady-state sustainable society with much less change will prevail. Photovoltaic technology directly capturing solar energy is a suitable icon or symbol of this scenario.

Energy descent involves a reduction of economic activity, complexity and population in some way as fossil fuels are depleted. The increasing reliance on renewable resources of lower energy density will, over time, change the structure of society to reflect many of the basic design rules, if not details, of pre-industrial societies. This suggests a ruralisation of settlement and economy, with less consumption of energy and resources and a progressive decline in human populations. Biological resources and their sustainable management will become progressively more important as fossil fuels and technological power declines. In many regions, forests will regain their traditional status as symbols of wealth. Thus the tree is a suitable icon of this scenario. Energy descent (like techno-explosion) is a scenario dominated by change, but that change might not be continuous or gradual. Instead it could be characterised by a series of steady states punctuated by crises (or mini-collapses) that destroy some aspects of industrial culture.

Collapse suggests a failure of the whole range of interlocked systems that maintain and support industrial society, as high-quality fossil fuels are depleted and/or climate change radically damages ecological support systems.[2] This collapse would be fast and more or less continuous without the restabilisations possible in energy descent. It would inevitably involve a major 'die-off' of human population and a loss of the knowledge and infrastructure necessary for industrial civilisation, if not more severe scenarios including human extinction and the loss of much of the planet's biodiversity.

VIEWS OF THE FUTURE

The views of academics and commentators about the future are coloured by their beliefs about the degree to which human systems are the product of our innate 'brilliance' that is independent from nature's constraints, or alternatively, beholden to biophysical deterministic forces. Those with plans and actions to shape the future (especially current power elites) tend to focus on scenarios where they see options for effective influence.

Over the last sixty years we have seen substantial achievements as well as many dreams and promises toward the techno-
explosion future that might free us from the constraints of
energetic laws or at least those of a finite planet. This belief
in perpetual growth has survived the scorn of mathemati-
cians explaining how constant exponential growth, even at
low rates, leads to explosion, literally.

> This belief in perpetual growth has survived
> the scorn of mathematicians explaining how
> constant exponential growth, even at low
> rates, leads to explosion, literally.

The term *negative growth* used by economists to describe
economic contraction shows that anything other than growth
is unthinkable. The dream of infinite growth from free energy
and colonising space have not been realised, despite the novel
and substantial contributions of computers and information
technology toward this goal.[3]

The unstated assumptions of 'business as usual'
On a more pragmatic and immediate scale, the reasons for
faith in future growth are rarely articulated but can be summa-
rised by a few common assumptions that seem to lie behind
most public documents and discussion of the future. These
do not represent specific or even recognised views of particular academics, corporate leaders or politicians, but are more
society-wide assumptions that are generally left unstated.
Among these assumptions are:

• Global extraction rates of important nonrenewable
   commodities will continue to rise.

Figure 4. Brasilia, capital of Brazil. Modernist hotel reflective of the rapid growth of the Brazilian economy as one of the emerging 'energy superpowers'. The optimism about the rapid growth of centralised political power led to the creation of this capital city out of the savannah woodlands of the Brazilian wilderness in the 1950s. The rapid growth and spread of technology, energy and political and economic power during the 1950s and 1960s cemented 'techno-explosion' as the default future that inevitably would lead to colonisation of space once the earthly frontiers had been developed.

- There will be no peaks and declines other than through high-energy substitution such as the historical transitions from wood to coal and from coal to oil.
- Economic activity, globalisation and increases in technological complexity will continue to grow.
- The geopolitical order that established the United States as the dominant superpower may evolve and change but will not be subject to any precipitous collapse such as happened to the Soviet Union.
- Climate change will be marginal or slow in its impacts on human systems, such that adaptation will not necessitate changes in the basic organisation of society.
- Household and community economies and social capacity will continue to shrink in both their scope and importance to society.[4]

Being more transparent about our assumptions becomes essential in times of turbulent
change and historical transition.

All of these assumptions are based on projections of past trends extending back over a human lifetime and drawing more broadly on patterns that can be traced to the origins of industrial civilisation and capitalism in Europe hundreds of years ago. Simply exposing these assumptions makes it clear how weak the foundations are for any planned response to the issue of energy transitions. Being more transparent about our assumptions becomes essential in times of turbulent change and historical transition if our aim is to empower personal and community action.

Since the environmental awareness and energy crises of the 1970s, we have had a parallel stream of thinking and modest achievements toward the techno-stability future that, in theory, is compatible with the limits of a finite planet. The principles and strategies of mainstream approaches to sustainability assume that the techno-stability long-term future is inevitable in some form, even if we go through some crises along the way. The focus is on how to make that transition from growth based on fossil energies to a steady state based on largely novel renewable sources.

Mainstream approaches to sustainability
assume that the techno-stability long-term
future is inevitable.

The tricky issue of dependence of the financial systems on continuous economic growth has been largely ignored or sidestepped by the assumption that the economy may be able to keep growing without using more and more materials and energy. The explosion of economic activity based on

Figure 5. Hydrogen-powered fuel-cell bus at the World Expo in Aichi, Japan, 2005. The concept of the hydrogen economy was popularised in the early 1990s as the next energy revolution that would deliver powerful and clean fuels from renewable sources. After massive investment in research by governments and corporations over nearly two decades, and with major rises in oil costs over the last five, the hydrogen economy seems more of a dream than ever. At Aichi, the dominant message of the World Expo shifted from that of the techno-explosion future to a softer sustainability message reflecting the techno-stability future.

financial services and information technology in the dominant economies during the early 1990s gave some credibility to this concept of the 'weightless economy', although it is now clear that globalisation simply shifted the consumption of resources to other countries to support this growth in the service economies.

Human capital

Much faith in both growth and steady-state scenarios rests on the observation that human ingenuity, technology, markets and social capital are at least as important in shaping history as raw energy and resources. The stunning power and spread of computers and information technology into all sectors of industrial society is seen to be as much as a product of human capital as it is of natural capital. The rise of the service economy

promised continued economic growth without using more
energy and materials. But these service economies and the
human capital that helped create them were themselves
created through flows of energy and resources. For example,
mass education, and especially mass post-secondary education,
is a very expensive investment in technical capacity and social
capital that has been possible because of economic wealth
from the extraction of cheap fossil energy and nonrenewable
resources.

In pre-industrial societies it was not possible to have so
many potential workers outside the productive economies of
agriculture and manufacturing, or to build the educational
infrastructure necessary for mass education. Human capital, in

> **Mass education has been possible because
> of the extraction of cheap fossil energy.**

the form of mass education, the media, democracy and other
characteristics of industrial culture, has greatly expanded the
apparent power of human rather than ecological factors in
determining our future. While these new forms of wealth are
clearly important, they are in reality 'stores' of high-quality
embodied fossil energy. Like more material forms of wealth,
they depreciate over time and must be used and renewed to
remain useful.

Much of the technological and economic innovation since
the oil shocks of the 1970s can be attributed to society's
capacity to draw on this human capital, and by further cycles
of reinvestment to build further human capital. Several factors
suggest the continuous growth in human capital and capacity
is an illusion.

First, much of this growth is in forms that are increasingly dysfunctional. For example, the increasingly sedentary life-style created by the computer and other innovation is requir-ing escalating expenditure in the health-care system and in the health and fitness industry to compensate for lifestyles that are incompatible with human biology.

Second, much of the economic growth since the energy crises of the 1970s has come through economical rational-ist policies such as privatisation. Many academics and social commentators have identified how much of the apparent economic growth has come at the cost of decline in many social indicators of well-being. We can think of this growth as being driven as much from mining (rather than maintaining) social capital as it has from mining the earth. For example, the privatisation of electricity and other utilities in many coun-tries including Australia has resulted in the loss of detailed knowledge and skill about the maintenance of infrastructure as workers are sacked, while budgets for maintenance, training and long-term planning have been cut to the bone. Gains in productivity and efficiency in the pursuit of profits have been achieved at the cost of resilience and long-term capacity.

One of the characteristics of a robust, enduring and mature civilisation is the capacity to consider the longer term and aim for desirable but achievable futures, but have fallback strategies and insurance policies to deal with surprise and uncertainty. Given the globalised nature of culture, knowledge and wealth, our industrial civilisation should have been able to devote resources to serious redesign strategies at the technological, infrastructural, organisational, cultural and personal levels that are able to respond to the potentials of all four long-term scenarios. Instead we see remarkably short-term behaviour and a cavalier disregard of the fate of future generations. While this is often explained as 'human nature' of fallible individu-als, this explanation should not apply to institutions such as

Figure 6. Nineteenth-century castle in the Czech village of Buzov with waste straw from field cropping in the foreground. The castle was a Romantic construction by an aristocrat. While it harks back to feudal times when castles were constructed from the wealth extracted from the land, tenant farmers and serfs, the money for this castle came from the early urban industrial wealth of central Europe, not the land. This bizarre expression of human capital is now a minor tourist attraction. The straw in the foreground, which was once collected for animal bedding in barns in the winter (and thus compost for the fields in spring) is now typically burned at the side of the field, leading to a decline in soil organic matter – a loss of critical biological capital. Biomass furnaces at district heating plants in Western Europe, and increasingly in the East, now use this straw as a fuel source. This 'green technology' entrenches the deprivation of the food-producing fields of the only source of organic matter able to sustain food production in the energy-descent future.

corporations, let alone governments. History and systems theory suggest that powerful and long-lived human institutions should embody longer-term cultural wisdom and capacity.

We can interpret the shortsighted nature of information and decision-making in our largest organisational structures as one of the many signs of cultural decay, reflecting the fact that our stocks of human capital may be declining just as our stock of natural capital is. Applying the concept of resource depletion to that of social capital in both affluent and poor countries over the last forty years is more than metaphorical.

This depletion suggests these less material forms of wealth may be subject to the same laws of energy and entropy that govern the natural capital of the earth, air and water.[5]

Consequently, we should be sceptical of the notion that innovation in technology and organisation is a continuously expanding human resource that we can rely on to solve ever-more complex challenges. This is not to say that given the right conditions humanity cannot rise to the energy-transition challenge we face. However, the conditions that could harness that human capacity are unlikely to include the continuation of endless economic growth, maintenance of current world power structures and the idolising of consumption. A smooth conversion to a steady-state economy running on renewable energy without massive geopolitical and economic crises is unlikely. In fact an increasing number of commentators recognise that we are already in the crisis that has been unfolding since the turn of the millennium.

Collapse

For a minority of intellectuals and ordinary citizens, unimpressed by the likelihood of techno-explosion or techno-stability, the logical future seems to be some kind of crisis leading to implosion and the collapse of civilisation. The old adage 'what goes up must come down' still has some truth, but several factors lead people to jump to the conclusion that the collapse scenario is inevitable without thinking about the possibilities of descent.

Several factors lead people to jump to the conclusion that the collapse scenario is inevitable without thinking about the possibilities of descent.

First, there is a long tradition of millennialism in Judeo-Christian culture that periodically leads to predictions of the 'end of the world as we know it' based on the idea that our current world is fundamentally flawed in some way. The simplicity and mostly incorrect nature of these past predictions suggest caution when considering current predictions of doom. The fable of the 'boy who cried wolf' is sometimes cited to suggest current concerns are also false alarms. But this history also has the effect of inoculating society against considering the evidence. Exposure to a small dose of millennialism leads to resistance to the effects of larger doses. Ironically, the point of the fable is that the threat of the wolf is real but that no one takes any notice because of past false alarms.

Another factor reinforcing this tendency of some to believe in collapse is the rapid rate of recent cultural change and the

> Ironically, the point of the 'boy who cried wolf' fable is that the threat of the wolf is real but that no one takes any notice because of past false alarms.

very short-term perspective of modern people despite the huge increase in knowledge about the distant past. Life in cities and suburbs surrounded by technology and sustained by reliable income and debt is 'normal' for many people in affluent countries, even though these features emerged only in the latter half of the twentieth century. If future change were to sweep away this way of life, many people would see this as 'the end of civilisation' even if these changes were quite modest from a historical perspective. For example, a return to the conditions of the Great Depression is clearly not 'the end of civilisation', but the idea that any downturn from the current peak of affluence represents 'the end of civilisation' is quite widely assumed. Perhaps this reflects the egocentric nature of modern mentality, where we consider our own survival and well-being as being more important than was perhaps felt by past generations. It may also be interpreted as an intuitive recognition that this peak of affluence, like peak oil, is a fundamental turning point that will break the illusion of the – more or less – continuous arrow of growth and progress into the distant future.

> There is substantial evidence that current, let alone projected, human populations cannot be sustained without fossil fuels.

The concept of overshoot in animal carrying capacity has been used by population ecologists to model past and potential future collapses in human populations.[6] There is substantial evidence that current, let alone projected, human populations cannot be sustained without fossil fuels. Historical evidence from the Black Death and other pandemics shows that societies can survive significant die-off in human numbers even if they do go through great setbacks and changes as a result. But, because human systems are now global in scope and integration, the more limited regional collapse of economies and civilisations in the past is not necessarily a model of the scale, intensity and likely recovery from any global collapse. Also, these societies were less complex, with less specialisation of critical functions. It is possible that loss of critical numbers of engineers, technologists, medical specialists or even large-scale farmers in a pandemic could cause modern industrial society to collapse very rapidly.

The consideration of collapse has been strongly influenced

by some ecological historians such as Catton, Diamond and Tainter. While Catton emphasises the concept of overshoot leading to severe collapse, Diamond emphasises the aspect of societal myopia leading to unnecessary collapse. Tainter provides a systemic view of how failure of energy-capture strategies leads to decline in complexity that can play out over centuries. In turn, the conditions for ordinary people may actually improve when the resources devoted to maintaining societal complexity are freed for meeting more basic needs. While all these perspectives and understandings are useful, I think the all-encompassing use of the term *collapse* is too broad a definition and inconsistent with our normal understanding of the term as a rapid and complete process. Historical examples of relatively complete and/or sudden civilisational collapse, from the Minoans in the eastern Mediterranean to the Maya in Mexico, are potential models for what could happen to global industrial civilisation. The best-documented historical case, that of the Roman Empire and, more broadly, Greco-Roman civilisation, suggests a more gradual and less complete decline process.

> The best documented historical case of collapse, that of the Roman Empire, suggests a more gradual and less complete decline process.

I don't want to underplay the possibility of a total and relatively fast global collapse of complex societies that we recognise as civilisation. I think this is a substantial risk, but the total-collapse scenario tends to lead to fatalistic acceptance, or alternatively, naïve notions of individual or family survivalist preparations. Similarly, the collapse scenario is so shocking

Figure 7. Ruins from the massive earthquake that devastated Valdivia, Chile, in 1960. This, and many other buildings that were never rebuilt, had been constructed on some of the 10,000 hectares that sank below sea level and became inundated to form vast wetland ecosystems. Over the following decades these wetlands developed such an abundance and diversity of bird life that they were listed in the Ramsar convention, an international agreement to conserve wetlands.

that it reinforces the rejection by the majority of even thinking about the future, thus increasing the likelihood of very severe energy descent, if not total collapse. Perhaps a majority of people think civilisational collapse is inevitable but think or hope that it won't happen in their lifetime. A more realistic assessment of the possibilities and adaptive responses to the collapse long-term scenario is possible only after a deep and nuanced understanding of the diverse possibilities and likelihoods of the energy-descent long-term scenario.

Energy descent: the ignored scenario
Public discussion of energy descent is generally seen as unrealistic, defeatist and politically counterproductive, although

many activists promoting sustainability strategies privately acknowledge that energy descent may be inevitable. I want to expand the systems approach to future energy transitions by focusing on the most ignored of the long-term scenarios for the following reasons.

- We do not have to believe that a particular scenario is likely before making serious preparations. For example, most people have fire insurance on their homes, not because they expect their primary asset to be destroyed by fire but because they recognise the severity of this unlikely event. Similarly, energy-descent scenarios, by their very nature, require more forethought and proactive planning than energy-growth or steady-state scenarios (to avert catastrophic consequences).
- The rapidly accumulating evidence on both climate change and the peaking of world oil supply, to name the two most important factors, makes some sort of energy descent increasingly likely despite the deep structural and psychological denial of this evidence.
- Permaculture principles and strategies (not necessarily by that name) such as relocalisation are likely to inform society-wide redesign and reorganisation in an energy-descent future. Since this scenario is the one in which permaculture is naturally at the fore, it is logical for those committed to permaculture to think more deeply about energy descent.[7]

Ecological modelling suggests an energy-descent path that could play out over a similar time frame to the industrial ascent era of 250 years. Historical evidence suggests a descent process that could involve a series of crises that provide stepwise transitions between consolidation and stabilisation phases that

Figure 8. Amish horse cart outside an SUV sales lot, Raleigh, North Carolina, 2005: a model for energy descent in more ways than the obvious. The Amish driver is likely to be a farmer, a symbol of the greater number of people who will be involved in food production, both domestically and commercially, in a future of less energy; in ironic contrast to the Burger King sign for fast food in the background.

could be more or less stable for decades before another crisis triggers another fall and then another restabilisation.[8]

There is a desperate need to recast energy descent as a positive process that can free people from the strictures and dysfunctions of growth economics and consumer culture. This is now apparent to many people around the world and is far more fundamental than a public relations campaign to paint a black sky blue.[9] It is a necessary process to provide a

> There is a desperate need to recast energy descent as a positive process that can free people from the strictures and dysfunctions of growth economics and consumer culture.

sense of hope and connection to fundamental human values expressed by every traditional culture throughout human history, among them that the pursuit of materialism is a false god.

One of the positive aspects of energy descent that is often overlooked is that it is a culture of continuous and novel change over many human generations. Ironically, the growth culture of the previous several hundred years provides us with some conceptual and cultural experience at dealing with change that traditional peoples in more stable societies lacked. We are now familiar with continuous change, that we must do something different from our parents' generation and that our children must do something different again. This may seem a small bright spot when considering the challenges of energy descent, but it is a real asset that we must harness if we are to deal with energy descent in the most graceful way possible.[10]

Permaculture

Serious and thoughtful responses to energy-descent futures over the last thirty years (from both sociological and ecological perspectives) have received limited attention academically.[11] In affluent countries, movements advocating low-energy life-styles such as permaculture have contributed mostly to action and changes at the fringes of society. Permaculture has been stress-tested in poor countries and in crisis situations, and as fossil-fuel depletion hits levels of affluence globally its relevance will likely increase radically.

Permaculture was one of the environmental design concepts to emerge from the 1970s debate over energy and resource availability and was founded on the assumption that the next energy transition would involve the re-emergence of biological systems as central to economics and society. The vision that informed permaculture design, teaching and action saw

relocalised food and renewable energy production, revitalised household and community economies, and bioregional
political structures establishing a permanent (i.e. sustainable)
human culture. The opportunistic use of fossil-fuelled wealth
and waste to fund the transition was an integral part of the
permaculture strategy. I see permaculture design generating more appropriate biological and human capital in ways
less demanding of physical resources and with low deprecia-
tion rates that are useful to a world of energy descent. In my
book *Permaculture: Principles and Pathways Beyond Sustainability*,
I explained the title in terms of the energy-descent future
undermining the steady-state notions inherent to most thinking about sustainability and even permaculture.

Permaculture has spread around the world but has an
extraordinary, perhaps unique, role in Australia as a concept,
a collection of design strategies, and as an environmental
movement. A definition is included in the dictionary, and it is
almost a household word.[12] As a 'brand' it carries a great deal
of good will but also much baggage and is generally regarded
in policy and planning circles as marginal to mainstream
decision-making. Some more thoughtful people recognise it
as tuned to a world of declining resources that will require
adaptive strategies quite different from those being pursued
currently.

Permaculture is already contributing to changing Australian
suburbs and lifestyle via bottom-up and organic processes.
Increasing community awareness of environmental issues
combined with rises in the cost of energy, water and food are
likely to lead to an explosion in permaculture-inspired activity in Australian cities, towns and rural landscapes. It is now
essential that academics, educators, activists, planners and policy
makers understand permaculture as both a factor in the social
and physical fabric of Australian society and a conceptual

Figure 9. 'Melliodora', central Victoria, 2004. View over poultry deep-litter yard, roof-runoff garden, and olive and fruit trees to house with solar clerestory showing above trees. This integration of building and garden agriculture, including animals and trees, is typical of small-scale intensive permaculture design that takes modest advantage of new and reused industrial materials and technology in combination with diverse plant and animal systems to rebuild biological capital of soil, water and living systems. The aim is to provide most basic human needs of water, food and energy from the immediate living environment. This is the starting point of a radical relocalisation strategy to enhance human engagement with nature, reduce environmental impact, and increase resilience in the face of declining energy and resource security.

framework for the organic redesign of society and culture for the energy–descent future in Australia as well as globally.

Not surprisingly, permaculture solutions have been more effectively applied in community and agricultural development work in poorer countries where energy descent has been an experienced reality. While these conditions can be understood in terms of inequitable distribution of resources rather than fundamental limits, they provide models for behaviour in response to energy descent. The most dramatic example is the role that permaculture strategies and techniques played in rapidly increasing urban food production as part of a multipronged strategy to avert famine in Cuba in the early 1990s following the collapse of the Soviet Union. What is particularly interesting about this model is that Cuba is a middle-income country with a long history of industrialised agriculture and an urbanised and dependent population similar to many affluent countries. Today Cubans have life expectancy and other indices of development comparable with the United States while using one-seventh the energy and resources.[13]

Permaculture is, intuitively, most relevant to the energy-descent scenarios in which there is a major decline in the power from nonrenewable resources, but many of the strategies are synergistic with those focused on appropriate responses to the techno-stability scenario, which demands a degree of relocalisation of food supply and other key economies and a shift from centralised to distributed energy sources.

Sometimes permaculture is understood as simply returning to traditional patterns from the past and is consequently criticised as impractical. While it is true that older, more traditional patterns of resource use and living provide some of the elements and inspiration for permaculture, it is certainly more than this. One way to understand permaculture is as a postmodern integration of elements from different traditions and modernity that involves continuous change and evolution. This builds on the human experience of continuous change rather than static tradition as well as the more recent emergence of design as a new literacy that allows us to effectively and efficiently respond to and redesign our environment and ourselves.[14]

CLIMATE CHANGE AND PEAK OIL

THE SIMULTANEOUS ONSET of climate change and the peaking of global oil supply represent unprecedented challenges driving this energy transition, but historians may look back with the verdict that the efforts at managing the transition were too little, too late. The immediacy of the problems undermines many of the options for longer-term restructuring around renewable energy and appropriate infrastructure. The systemic interlocking of human and environmental systems suggests that other apparently independent crises, from the psychological to the geopolitical, are being drawn together to reinforce a historic inflection point.

CLIMATE CHANGE

While peak oil has remained a concept at the fringe of public debate and policy, climate change has gathered speed as the key environmental issue demanding attention alongside more traditional concerns about economics and security. The creation of the Intergovernmental Panel on Climate Change (IPCC) in 1988 reflected the scientific consensus in the mid-1980s that increasing atmospheric carbon dioxide was caused by human emissions, but the realisation that climate change was already happening began to take shape in the 1990s, and by 2007 even political leaders in the United States and Australia (who had become infamous for denying climate change) began to accept it as a reality. It has been the increase

in drought and extreme weather events more than increases
in average temperatures or subtle ecological changes that have
spurred the political and public realisation that climate change
is already happening. The focus has shifted from impacts on
nature to impacts on humanity.

Strategies for reducing greenhouse-gas emissions have
become almost synonymous with the sustainability concept.
New financial instruments such as carbon trading have developed despite the uncertainty about international agreements

Figure 10. Thunderstorm cell over New Guinea, 2005. Rapid growth in air travel has
been one of the signposts of very rapid growth in greenhouse gas emissions that
have exceeded the worst-case scenarios of the early reports on climate change by
the IPCC. The aviation industry is also one of the most vulnerable to peak-oil-induced
escalation in fuel costs. It appears that rising costs will cut emissions faster than international agreements and consumer restraint.

to underpin and sustain them. Renewable energy sources have grown significantly, especially in countries with the most progressive responses to climate change. At the same time, geological sequestration of carbon dioxide has been strongly promoted as a way to allow coal-fired power stations to continue to provide the bulk of the world's electric power without creating climate chaos. The nuclear industry has been recast as an environmental saviour. Despite all the focus on the issue, the emissions of greenhouse gases worldwide have continued to parallel economic growth. Consequently the emissions increases have been higher than even the worst-case (business as usual) scenarios produced in the earlier reports by the IPCC.

> Hansen's report suggests that the onset of severe impacts from climate change is now inevitable, even if there is a huge worldwide effort at mitigation.

The most recent evidence on climate change is showing that the rate of onset of warming in the Arctic makes the IPCC's fourth report look incompetent in its failure to be alarmist enough.[1]

Greenland ice-cap melting and sea-ice retreat are now occurring far faster than expected. The IPCC's ponderous processes for its reports have ignored this new evidence. James Hansen's research suggests that sea-level rises could be 5 metres (16 feet) by 2100 rather than the 0.5 metre (1.6 feet) used in the IPCC's fourth report. This suggests that the onset of severe impacts from climate change is now inevitable, even if there is a huge worldwide effort at mitigation.

There is also very little evidence that mitigation within

the context of modern affluent society will radically reduce greenhouse-gas emission in any case. Most of the increases in efficiency and other gains through technology have been countered by increases in emissions elsewhere. This may appear to be due to the small scale and spread of these gains, but there is a more fundamental problem that is known to systems theorists as the 'rebound effect' or the 'Jevons paradox'. A gain in resource efficiency in one part of a system is immediately used to drive growth in another part. For example, savings made by a householder in reducing home-heating costs are typically being spent on something like an overseas holiday.

> Economic recession is the only proven mechanism for a rapid reduction of greenhouse gas emissions.

This suggests that without radical behavioural and organisational change that would threaten the foundations of our growth economy, greenhouse-gas emissions along with other environmental impacts will not decline. Economic recession is the only proven mechanism for a rapid reduction of greenhouse-gas emissions and may now be the only real hope for maintaining the Earth in a habitable state.

Further, most of the proposals for mitigation, from Kyoto to the feverish efforts to construct post-Kyoto solutions, have been framed in ignorance of peak oil. As Richard Heinberg has argued recently, proposals to cap carbon emissions annually, and allowing them to be traded, rely on the rights to pollute being scarce relative to the availability of the fuel.[2] Actual scarcity of fuel may make such schemes irrelevant.

ENERGY RESERVES
AND PRODUCTION PEAKS

Most of the comparative discussion about energy resources has focused on 'proven, probable and possible reserves'. These are economic concepts about what can be profitably extracted using current technology and prices. Banks lend massive amounts of money to develop energy projects over long periods with risks of price collapses that can reduce or eliminate profits. The proven reserves represent assets that can be considered as collateral by the lender. There is a long history of 'reserve growth' of proven reserves. While some of this is due to technology improvement, and more recently price rises, very little is due to finding more oil. Most of this growth is simply due to shifting reserves from the 'probable' to the 'proven' category and is driven by reporting policies and regulations.

Nationalisation of oil reserves in the 1970s allowed OPEC countries to report reserve growth with less scrutiny by Western banks, and in the 1980s radical upward revision of reserve figures was made without finding any more oil. This hopeless corruption of reserve figures, of arguably the most important set of accounts in the world, was not exposed until the late 1990s with the work of Campbell and Laherrere, which set off the current debate about peak oil.[3] It is still yet to be accepted or acknowledged by governments or inter-governmental agencies such as the International Energy

> The collective myopia on the part of the intelligentsia is all the more stunning because it has been increasing rates of energy production that have underpinned economic growth.

Figure 11. An oil well jack pump, Cuba 2007. This type of pump technology has been widely used to extract oil from low-yielding onshore oilfields. In recent years the jack pump has become a symbol associated with the concept of peak oil.

Agency, charged with providing transparent and accurate information on energy resources.[4]

The debate about peak oil has also highlighted the confusion in economic and political discourse about the importance of production rates and their potential to keep expanding. This collective myopia on the part of the intelligentsia is all the more stunning because it has been increasing rates of energy production (not reserve growth) that have underpinned economic growth. The orthodox view that healthy reserves, by themselves, can ensure expanding production has been shown to be false.

Similarly, the conventional wisdom that coal reserves are so great that we can expand coal-based electricity with or without carbon sequestration and make liquid fuel from coal is now being widely challenged.[5] As with oil, we see that reserve figures are of dubious reliability, and large reserves do not mean that production rates can necessarily increase. The slow rate of increase in oil production from the Canadian tar

sands, despite massive investment, heroic efforts in engineering and logistics (and massive environmental damage), proves
that large reserves do not necessarily lead to high production
rates. The fact that Canada, overnight, became the nation with
the largest oil reserves in the world because it was allowed to
classify its tar sands as oil highlights the arbitrary nature of the
reserve concept.[6] It is highly likely that nowhere near enough
fossil fuels can be mined fast enough to generate the worst-
case emission scenarios of the IPCC. It is just unfortunate that
climate change seems to be happening at much lower levels
of atmospheric carbon dioxide than predicted in those same
models.

> The evidence on peak oil is gathering so
> fast that it is now certain that the world has
> already peaked in the production of cheap
> (conventional) oil.

The evidence on peak oil is gathering so fast that it is now
certain that the world has already peaked in the production
of cheap (conventional) oil and that the peak production of
'crude plus condensate' (the standard measure of oil) may
have already passed despite vigorous debunking of peak oil
that continues in policy circles and the media.[7] The steady
climb in prices for eight years should have been enough to
lift production if that were possible. The impacts of peak oil
are unfolding all around us in the world, but they are being
regularly interpreted in the media as caused by more familiar (above-ground) factors such as terrorism, oil nationalism,
corporate greed or incompetence, speculators and so on. The
combination of rolling crises and obfuscation of the issues
is leading to confusion and inappropriate responses (from

oil wars to biofuels made from agricultural crops) that are compounding the problems.

The debate among peak-oil analysts has now shifted from 'when' to 'at what rate' the world will decline after we move off the current plateau in production. The decline rates in the UK and Mexico have provided progressively stronger evidence that the application of modern management and technology in oil production, while delaying peak, ultimately leads to faster decline rates than had been expected (based on past rates of national decline). If these higher decline rates follow through into global decline, then mitigation and adaptation strategies, without economic collapse, will be very difficult. Given the accelerating consumption of natural gas and coal we should assume peak production of both will quickly follow oil peak.

COLLAPSING OIL EXPORTS

Another factor is already accelerating the impact of global peak on the importing countries. Almost all of the oil-producing countries have rapidly growing economies driven by large oil revenues and in many cases rapidly growing populations. Internal consumption in these countries is ensuring that after peak, the rate of exports declines much faster than production. Indonesia is a prime example, where all of these factors have combined to make this once-major exporter a net importer of oil. Mexico is another major producer showing the same pattern, while the two largest producers and exporters, Saudi Arabia and Russia, may also see exports collapse due to rising internal consumption. Global economic growth may continue for some years in oil- and resource-rich countries, but not in the importing

Figure 12. Shipping-container loading terminal, Melbourne, with General Motors car factory across the Yarra River, 2003, signifying the globalisation of trade that, given the most recent, and perhaps last, great boost in economic efficiency, was predicated on very cheap energy. The rising cost of intercontinental shipping is threatening to reverse the globalisation of manufacturing. Resource nationalism and insecurity may combine with global recession to drive a retreat from global trade faster than actual energy costs.

countries that have been used to affluence and continuous economic growth for longest.[8]

Alternatively, a constant state of corruption, dysfunction and/or open war in oil-exporting countries can have the effect of enforcing exports in the face of shortages at home. Although this appears counterintuitive, the failure of functional governance in the national interest combined with a shattered or stunted economy reduces the capacity of the national market to pay for oil and allows foreign oil companies to gain favourable concessions and military protection from corrupt governments. Aspects of this scenario are at work to maintain the flow of oil from Nigeria and Iraq to the United States and other large importers.

Thus, we can see both the collapsing-exports and enforced-export scenarios unfolding simultaneously as the major expression of the struggle for declining production. This suggests, at the very least, massive shifts in geopolitical and economic power over the next few years, even if global growth continues.

NET ENERGY RETURN

An even more fundamental issue is that of net energy return. It takes energy to get energy. Fossil fuels have been such an abundant source of concentrated energy that the investment of energy we make in exploration, mining, transportation and processing has been relatively small. Even when we consider all the energy embodied in equipment and infrastructure, the net energy return or profit has been very high. Adding all the energy and resources needed to train and support all the engineers and other employees in the energy industries still leaves a huge net energy profit, which explains why the oil industry has been such a profitable one. However, now that

This decline in net energy yield results in an increasing proportion of society's real wealth being devoted to the energy-harvesting sectors of the economy, leaving less and less for all other sectors.

we have passed the peak of production of conventional oil, the net energy yield from new projects tapping the heavy, deep ocean, the Arctic, and small remaining amounts in old oilfields, using advanced recovery methods, is less and less.

Other resource-extraction sectors of the economy such as

mining, fishing and forestry have an escalating energy demand as poorer, lower-quality and more remote resources are exploited. Mining and metal-processing currently use about 10 per cent of the world energy supply. This energy use is expanding rapidly as lower-quality ore bodies are mined to meet growth in demand and depletion of better-quality ores.[9]

The idea that biofuels or coal-to-liquids will simply replace oil and gas the way oil and gas have replaced wood and coal shows an astonishing degree of ignorance of the concept of net energy. When we moved from wood to coal and then to oil, the increase in power available to humanity was not just from the increasing quantity of energy, but also from the increasing quality. The quantity is easily measured in joules (heat energy released), but the quality is something scientists are more confused about. It is widely accepted by scientists that energy quality is real and determines the usefulness of energy, but without an agreed way to measure quality it is largely ignored.

The net energy concept is just beginning to surface in media and policy circles as a way to assess alternative energy sources and strategies, especially in the debate over corn etha-nol in the United States. While different methods of account-ing for net energy produce substantially different net energy profit figures, they all show a pattern of higher returns for current and past sources of fossil and renewable energy than new ones. Economic power and profit from past development of different energy sources also reflects these general patterns revealed by net energy calculation methods. This suggests they can be used to predict real economic impacts of future energy systems.

The declining net energy yields of our energy resources results in an increasing proportion of society's real wealth being devoted to the energy-harvesting sectors of the economy,

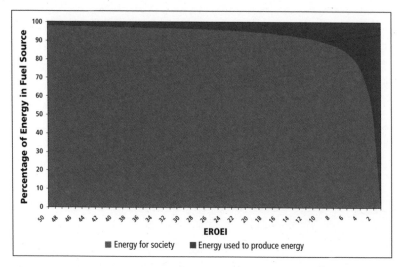

Figure 13. The dramatic effect as energy return on energy invested falls below 10 is illustrated by this graph.

leaving less and less for all other sectors. The implications of declines in net energy from new resources are so shocking that there is much confusion and denial about the concept of net energy.

The promotion by the US Department of Agriculture of research showing an energy return on energy invested (EROEI) of 1.6 for corn ethanol as a 'good result' indicates how the understanding of these issues is very poor, even by the scientifically literate.[10] A society based on an energy source of this quality would be constantly investing 62 per cent of its energy back into the energy industry (the 1 in 1.6), leaving only the remaining 38 per cent of the total energy in society for everything else – health, education, culture, food production, law, leisure and so on. Our modern industrial society has been fuelled by energy sources with EROEI rates as high as 100 and no lower than 6 (requiring between 1 per cent and 17 per cent of the wealth created being invested to get the yield).

Ironically, conventional economics is blind to this shift

because one type of economic transaction is considered as good as another, so growth in the energy sector at the expense of, say, personal consumption is not seen as indicative of any fundamental problem.

My own tracking of these issues over the last thirty years leads me to the conclusion that the next energy transition is to sources with lower energy-production rates and lower net energy yield, which in turn will drive changes in human economy and society that are without precedent since the decline and/or collapse of previous complex civilisations such as the Mayan and the Roman.

The most sophisticated method of evaluating net energy, with the longest history of development, is *emergy* accounting, developed by Howard Odum and colleagues.[11] It has informed my own development of permaculture principles and strategies over the last thirty years, but unfortunately it remains unknown or at best misunderstood in academic and policy circles. *Emergy* accounting includes ways of measuring energy quality (called 'transformity'). This makes it possible to account for small quantities of very high-quality energy in technology and human services that undermine many of the more optimistic assessments of alternative energy sources including biomass, nuclear and solar.

To test the relative impact of net energy compared with declines in energy production rates, I used a recent assessment of global energy production to 2050 by Paul Chefurka that was published and discussed on The Oil Drum website.[12] The study was well referenced and its assumptions and methodology were clear. It took account of likely reductions from oil, gas and coal but included reasonably optimistic figures for future production from renewables and nuclear. It shows a peak in total energy production at about 2020 followed by a decline to 70 per cent of 2005 production by 2050. This is a very serious

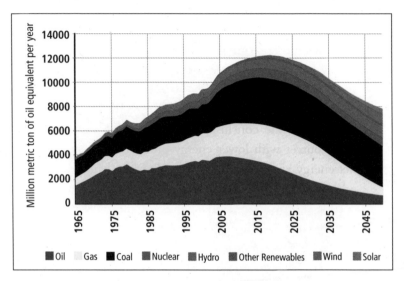

Figure 14. The graph models gross energy availability. Because of decreasing net energy yields of many of the above resources, actual available energy for society will likely decrease more dramatically. Reproduced with permission from Paul Chefurka.

reduction given an expected global population of nine billion. Figure 14 shows the key production projections, and Figures 15 and 16 the energy-mix pie charts from the study.

Using published emergy accounting studies[13] I multiplied these current and projected global energy sources by their net emergy yield ratios. This shows that the energy quality of the 2050 energy mix will be 58 per cent of the 2005 energy mix. This suggests that declining net energy is a greater factor than projected declines in production. Multiplying these factors together suggests that real energetic power available to humanity will be 40 per cent of current yields. This does not allow for the energetic cost of carbon sequestration (still unknown) to ameliorate the otherwise disastrous impacts on the climate of the increased use of coal.

Further, it does not take account of decline (or increase) in the average net energy return for a particular source. While

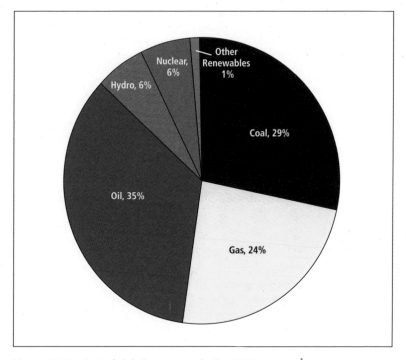

Figure 15. Pie chart of global energy production 2005. Reproduced with permission from Paul Chefurka.

it is possible that net energy return from newer renewable sources (such as solar and even wind) could conceivably improve with time, it is more likely that they will decline as the embedded fossil energy contribution (to the new energy sources) declines. What is more certain is that net energy return from fossil fuels including coal will decline, so that the

The net energy return from fossil fuels including coal will decline, so that the calculation of about 40 per cent of current net energy being available by 2050 is still optimistic.

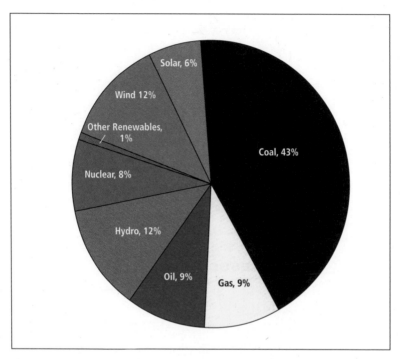

Figure 16. Pie chart of estimated global energy production 2050 based on assumptions in study by Paul Chefurka. Reproduced with permission from Paul Chefurka.

calculation of about 40 per cent of current net energy being available by 2050 is still optimistic. A new evaluation of the net energy return of gas production in North America using a methodology developed by Cleverland and Costanza suggests net energy return is in the process of a collapse so severe that net energy yield from gas in Canada will effectively fall to almost nothing by 2014 and that similar results apply to US production.[14] This is very different from the official view that claims the United States has eighty-six years of production at 2004 levels based on production-to-reserves ratios.

The great optimism in industry circles about future production from unconventional gas resources such as coal seam methane in eastern Australia or the Marcellus Shale in the

United States may reflect the potential for growing industrial activity supported by rapidly rising prices, but where production rate and net energy return to society decline. This result would be good for investors right up to the point where the industry collapses.

The implications of some of this information are so shocking that the naïve and simplistic idea that we are running out of oil and gas (rather than just peaking in production) may be closer to the truth than even the most pessimistic assessments of peak-oil proponents a decade ago.

ASSOCIATED ISSUES

Many other factors beyond climate change and peak oil are increasing the stress on global ecosystems and humanity, making some form of energetic descent, if not collapse, seem inevitable. A few of the more fundamental ones need at least a mention.

Critical materials depletion

Accelerating economic growth and energy extraction over the last decade has greatly increased depletion of other essential nonrenewable resources, especially phosphates for food production and nonferrous metals for industry.[15] Almost all the unfolding plans and projects for energy transition beyond oil will place more demand on these depleting resources. For example, the demand for nickel-steel alloys required for high-pressure natural gas pipelines is pushing up the price of nickel and further depleting the remaining stocks. As lower-quality deposits of critical materials are tapped, energy demands for extraction and processing will escalate dramatically and production rates will fall. The title of Richard Heinberg's latest book, *Peak Everything*, sums up the situation.[16]

Water depletion

Water is the most abundant resource used by humanity, but the growing demand is so vast that the limits once specific to a bioregion are now being expressed at the global scale. Although I don't subscribe to the view that global water shortage will constrict global growth before or more severely than liquid fuel supplies, the global water crisis is already quite severe. Even if we attribute the most dramatic impacts of droughts directly to climate change, other factors are independently contributing to the water crisis. The loss of wetlands, perennial vegetation and forests as well as soil humus are all reducing the capacity of catchments and soils to catch and store water between periods of rain, which in turn escalates demand for irrigation. Increasing affluence is directly and indirectly increasing water consumption, especially through intensive livestock husbandry dependent on irrigated fodder crops. The extraction of groundwater beyond recharge rates, including huge reserves laid down after the last ice age, makes many water resources as depletable as fossil fuels, giving rise to the term *fossil water*. Finally, the decline in water quality is increasing death and illness from water-borne diseases and demand for expensive water filtration and treatment, as well as bottled-water supplies.

Food supply

The unfolding global food crisis can be largely attributed to the manifold interactions and secondary effects of energy costs and climate change, including droughts and bad seasons, biofuel demand, and escalating costs of (energy-intensive) fertilisers, pesticides and irrigation. Other factors exacerbating

the crisis include rising affluence, increasing demand (especially for beef and cotton), past low prices destroying farming as a livelihood, and failure of the land-reform agenda in
most countries. Fixing these secondary factors is technically
possible, but seems unlikely. There is also evidence that agriculture is running up against fundamental yield limits for our
main crops that, despite all the promises, genetic engineering
has failed to break through. Widespread application of organic
methods and permaculture design, especially when applied to
small-scale systems, could reduce the impact of the crisis, but
this will not be simple or quick.

Population pressures

The continued growth in human numbers is now pushing
well beyond that which could be sustainably supported without fossil fuels. Although affluence, conflict and other human-
created factors are multiplying the impact of population, there
are structural factors that make the large and growing human
population more important than it might otherwise be. The
total size of the human population, its density of settlement in
cities, and the constant interchange of microbes due to travel
and trade are all powerful factors increasing the likelihood
of new and old diseases creating pandemics on an unprecedented scale.

Financial instability

The accelerating growth and concentration of debt and financial assets, especially in the housing and derivatives markets, is
destabilising the global economy. The virtual impossibility that
future growth in the real economy could ever be large enough
to justify those debts and assets suggests a major and enduring economic contraction in the near future. Alternatively,
we may see the financial crisis in the United States trigger a

collapse similar to that which happened in the Soviet Union. As this book was going to press, the global financial crisis has been bigger news than the landslide presidential election victory of Obama in the US. There is a substantial chance that the desperate attempts by central banks to reinflate the US and European economies will fail, making a depression of greater magnitude than the so called Great Depression a likely outcome. On the other hand, if the reinflation is successful then rising demand for oil and other commodities will create new price spikes that will quickly precipitate the next crash. Whatever happens in the future, the fundamental cause of this latest economic recession is the same as four of the last five global recessions: a sudden rise in oil prices. As always, energy fuels the economy while financial activity increasingly represents little more than steam, smoke, froth and bubble which confuses the picture. If China, India, Russia and other growing economies survive relatively unscathed, completely new global power and economic systems could emerge quite quickly.

Psychosocial limits to affluence

The psychosocial limits of affluent consumer culture suggest that multigenerational mass affluence may burn itself out in a few generations, through dysfunctional behaviour, addictions and depression.[17] While the 'Roaring Twenties' in affluent countries gave some examples of the excesses of affluence that were swept away by the Great Depression and Second World War, the three generations of affluence since then have stimulated lifestyles and behaviours that are amplifying unsustainable resource consumption to new heights. The onset of severe psychosocial dysfunction in the long-affluent Western world could be as powerful a force as instability in the financial system.

Species extinction

The accelerating rate of species extinctions suggests humans have initiated a wave of extinctions on the scale of the asteroid that is believed to be the cause of the mass extinction that wiped out the dinosaurs sixty-five million years ago. Apart from the ethical and psychological issues involved, it is hard to predict how and when this will result in major adverse impacts on humanity other than to recognise that it is eroding the genetic base that we will increasingly depend on in the future, as well as increasing ecological instability that is undermining our ability to produce food.[18]

Despite the severity of these and other associated problems, I see climate change and peak oil as the most fundamental ones for the following reasons.

- They are both inevitable consequences of the accelerating use of fossil fuels, the undeniable primary factor in creating the explosion of human numbers, cultural complexity and impacts on nature.
- They both appear to be generating immediate and severe threats to humanity.
- They both show a long-term pattern of accelerating intensity.
- They both contribute directly or indirectly to the impact of the other serious problems threatening humanity and nature.

To suggest that the next energy transition will fall well short of the past patterns of human collective expectations is a gross understatement. My quick overview of evidence with regard to the most critical issues suggests we need to refocus our assumptions about the future around energy descent while developing the psychosocial and eco-technical capacity to respond to the range of possible scenarios that we could face.

While continued efforts to better understand the rate of onset of climate change and the decline in oil production are very useful, an equally important task is to understand how these factors will combine to create differing futures.

DESCENT SCENARIOS

SCENARIO PLANNING

THE SYSTEMS APPROACH to the energy-descent future can be taken further by using a scenario-planning model that combines two fundamental and largely independent variables that generate four scenarios, one for each of the quadrants of a conceptual graph. Scenarios in this context are plausible and internally consistent stories about the future that help organisations and individuals to achieve a broad and open-ended adaptability to inherent unpredictability.

In classic corporate scenario planning the two variables might be the growth rate in the wider economy and the regulatory framework that constrains or encourages business. But it was the use of scenario planning by the Shell oil company that first brought the method to prominence. Prior to the oil crises, scenario planning had been used to identify a range of scenarios that could threaten the company, including oil embargo. Working through the indicators and consequences, the company was able quickly and proactively to respond to the crisis more effectively than the other oil corporations.

Climate change and oil-production decline are the variables I use as the primary drivers in creating the four energy-descent scenarios, because I believe these are the strongest forces shaping human destiny over the twenty-first century and beyond. Consequently they are central to consideration of the energy transition across nations and cultures and in both urban and rural environments.

INTERACTION OF PEAK OIL
AND CLIMATE CHANGE

Although both variables are caused by collective human behaviour and potentially can be ameliorated by human behaviour, they arise from geological and climatic limits beyond human control. The debate over amelioration versus adaptation to climate change is often portrayed as a potent moral choice between burning coal and accepting a changed world, or a shift to renewable energy to save nature. The emerging evidence suggests that this choice was one that humanity collectively fudged in the 1980s.

Similarly, the actions necessary to make an orderly transition from oil to other energy sources have been assessed as taking at least two decades.[1] Again, society had the evidence from the peaking of US oil production in 1970, but with the return of cheap oil in the 1980s the energy problem appeared to have simply gone away owing to 'better' economic policies. Now climate change is accelerating and peak oil is upon us.

As well as having to adapt to both of these new realities, we also grapple with the interactions, both positive and negative. The accelerating shift to increased dependence on natural gas is often portrayed as a positive reduction in carbon intensity, but this is simply accelerating the depletion of our children's remaining inheritance of high-quality transportation fuel. Similarly, projects developing tar sands and other low-grade sources of oil massively increase greenhouse-gas emissions. Perhaps more surprising to some, the huge push in the United States and Europe to make biofuels from corn and oil-seed crops is increasing land degradation and resource consumption and contributing to driving up the cost of grains and oil seeds. Many authorities are warning of global famine due to climate and energy crisis factors (including biofuels) coming together.[2]

> We can build local resilience no matter where we live, at the same time as we make the greatest contribution to reducing greenhouse gas emissions.

The low EROEI of biofuels, especially corn-based ethanol, suggests biofuels may be a way to deplete natural gas while degrading agricultural land and starving the world's poor.

On the other hand, radical reductions in consumption due to transformative lifestyle change, creative re-use of wastes generated by industrial and consumer systems, and a shift to truly productive work within revitalised home and community economies show how we can build local resilience and capacity to adapt to the destructive change at the same time as we make the greatest contribution to reducing greenhouse gas emissions and fossil-fuel depletion rates. While this strategy would be most productive and effective in the most affluent countries, it has increasing relevance worldwide.[3]

The reluctance to seriously consider positive reductions in consumption in public debate about climate solutions could be swept away by the unfolding global energy and food crisis. Developing some of the harder and longer-term ecological and modest technological adaptations to ongoing and relentless energy descent will take decades to have widespread impacts (as do all high-energy, high-tech centralised approaches), but radical and rapid human behavioural change is possible and even likely (given the right psychosocial conditions). The emerging energy and economic crisis will make these reductions a reality, with or without a planned and creative response.

The alternative scenarios I have constructed provide more detail about how the energy-descent future might evolve over the next few decades rather than the hundreds of years of the long-term scenarios. In addition to combining the effects of slow or rapid oil-production decline, and slow or rapid global warming, they cover a very broad spectrum of human possibilities that can be recognised by various symptoms and signs in different places in the world today. They are all energy-descent scenarios in that they depict possible futures with progressively declining net energy. This must be understood against the historical background in which energy use per capita globally has been on a bumpy plateau for thirty years after the previous thirty years of rapid growth per capita from the end of World War II. The graph in Figure 17, from the previously mentioned study by Paul Chefurka, suggests worldwide per capita energy use may continue to rise to about 1.7 metric tons of oil equivalent (toe) by 2020 before falling to 0.9 toe by 2050.[4]

However, my own rough calculations using net energy ratios (from Odum) to convert these undifferentiated joules of energy in more appropriate measures of net energy per person

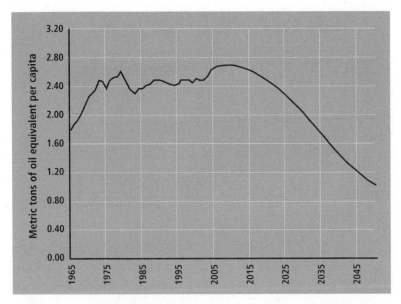

Figure 17. Average global energy production per capita from 1965 to 2045. Reproduced with permission from Paul Chefurka.

suggest the world is already past the peak in net energy per person and will soon be into absolute global net energy decline.

THE FOUR ENERGY-DESCENT AND CLIMATE-CHANGE SCENARIOS

In this section, four energy-descent scenarios are considered, each emerging from a combination of either fast or slow oil decline and either mild or severe climate change over the next ten to thirty years. I've labelled these:

- Brown tech (slow oil decline, fast climate change)
- Green tech (slow oil decline, slow climate change)
- Earth steward (fast oil decline, slow climate change)
- Lifeboats (fast oil decline, fast climate change).

Figure 18. The four global climate-change and energy-descent scenarios.

While the characterisation of the four scenarios is difficult and inevitably speculative, the scenarios do provide a framework for considering how peak oil and climate change could interact to reshape global and local energy resources, settlement patterns, economy and governance. They also provide some insight into what could be effective responses for aware activists to secure their own and their families' future while contributing to society in a positive way. Those responses might include potentially effective policies that could be adopted by forms of government that might be functional and effective in each of the scenarios.[5]

Finally, these scenarios clarify the relevance of permaculture principles in a world of energy descent and focus our attention on the strengths and weaknesses of various strategies in adapting to the differing scenarios.

Brown tech: top-down constriction
Slow energy-decline rates, severe climate-change symptoms

The brown-tech world is one in which the production of oil declines after its peak between 2005 and 2010 at about 2 per cent per annum and the subsequent peak and decline of natural gas is also relatively gentle, but the severity of global warming symptoms is at the extreme end of current mainstream scientific predictions. In this scenario strong, even aggressive, national policies and actions prevail to address both the threats and the opportunities from energy peak and climatic change. The political system could be characterised as corporatist or fascist (which Mussolini described as a merger of State and corporate power).

The tendency in existing systems for massive centralised

investment by corporations and governments gives priority to getting more energy out of lower-grade nonrenewable resources (e.g. tar sands, coal and uranium) and biofuels from industrial agriculture and forestry. 'Breakthrough' technologies provide the constant promise of a better future, but much of the investment in energy harvesting accelerates global warming, at least in the short term.

At the same time the cost of defending or replacing urban infrastructure threatened by storms and future sea-level rise consumes more resources, while droughts and chaotic

Figure 19. Sea walls on the water front, Havana, Cuba, destroyed by hurricanes and concrete cancer, 2007. In the brown-tech scenario, aging urban coastal infrastructure combined with falling government budgets leads to great impacts from increasing natural disasters driven by increased storm frequency and intensity plus sea-level rises of more than a metre per decade. In some areas huge investment is spent on new infrastructure to protect urban areas that have no long-term prospects.

Figure 20. Petrochemical plant, Altona, Victoria, 2003. In the brown-tech scenario, the petrochemical industry expands its use of low-quality feedstocks such as heavy oil and coal with high prices and government incentives to maintain supplies of fuel, plastics and chemicals for essential industries and new infrastructure.

seasonal changes reduce food production from large-scale and small-scale agriculture.

Flows of energy from more expensive sources such as tar sands, deep-ocean oil, gas-to-liquids and coal-to-liquids slow the decline in fuels from crude oil. This transition requires a huge mobilisation of the technical and managerial capacity held mostly by global corporations, along with the financial, legal and military security that only sovereign governments can provide. This resource nationalism by governments breaks down free trade and the faith in international markets that underpins the global economy.[6]

By 2007, we had already seen the shift from a buyer's to a seller's market for energy cascading through all commodities markets and reshaping geopolitical relations.[7] The profits from both nonrenewable resources and large-scale industrial agriculture rise on the back of high commodity prices, reversing many of the economic patterns and trends of recent decades. The wealth of farmers and miners as well as corporations and

Figure 21. Cultivation for large-scale vegetable production, Ventura, California, 2005. In the brown-tech scenario, increased aridity and unreliable water supplies reduce production of grains and other staples causing governments to give priority to fuel, fertiliser and technology for agribusiness to ensure food security for large urban populations. Demand for fruits and vegetables from centralised market systems declines owing to increasing poverty and more self-reliance on home and community gardens. Some land previously growing high-value horticultural crops for national and global markets is converted to production of grains and other staples.

nations in control of these resources increases even as depletion reduces the flows of resources, and climate change causes chaos in farming and land management.

The demand for biofuels in affluent countries reduces world food stocks and raises prices to levels that result in famine and chaos in many poor countries unable to sustain subsidies for staple food.[8] In other countries, food riots by the poor force governments to pay for escalating subsidies. The wealth left over for education, health and so on collapses. Wars to secure fuel and food increase and refocus public attention on external threats. In richer countries, consumer-led economic growth falters or is actively shut down by government policies to focus limited resources on food, fuel and climate security. Some type of global economic depression unfolds from the combined effects of high energy and food prices, super-

power contest, resource nationalism and the fragility of the
financial system.

Rapid onset of climate change also tends to support
centralised nationalist systems for several reasons. First, the
consequences of chaotic weather, food-supply problems, radical land-use change and abandonment of marginal land leads
to demands for strong government action to protect people
from high food and fuel costs, natural disasters, the consequences of strong action by other nations and mass migration by displaced people. Rates of urbanisation increase as the
impacts of climate change and withdrawal of government-
supported services in more remote rural regions accelerates.

A decline of the middle class already evident in many
Western countries accelerates, leading to discontent and
suppression by governments, including internment camps
either for migrants or for homeless people.[9] Strong approaches
to population control, even forced sterilisation, are introduced
in some countries.

A series of short but intense international conflicts confirm
major shifts in global power balances while accelerating
resource depletion. Control of nonrenewable fossil fuel and
mineral resources remains critical, while the (relative) importance of distributed renewable wealth from agriculture and
forestry continues to decline as the climate deteriorates, especially in my home country of Australia, where greater severity
of droughts hits hard. With food supply under threat, fossil

A decline of the middle class already evident
in many Western countries accelerates,
leading to discontent and suppression by
governments, including internment camps
either for migrants or for homeless people.

Figure 22. Banner in antiglobalisation demonstration, Melbourne, 2000, that reads 'Permaculture: Local Solutions to Global Problems'. In the brown-tech scenario, permaculture and other grassroots approaches to sustainable resource use remain relatively marginal to the dominant economic and political decision-making.

fuels and other resources are redirected from personal mobility and consumption to intensive factory farming in greenhouses and other controlled environments, mostly clustered around urban centres and managed by agribusiness corporations.

Desalination and other high-energy ways to maintain water-supply systems are built at huge cost and further increase demand for energy. The threat of sea-level rises leads to large-scale urban redevelopment driven by strong government policies. Some very bold initiatives for energy-efficient medium-density urban development and public-transportation infrastructure are funded. A key characteristic of this scenario is the sense of divide between the falling numbers of 'haves' dependent on a job in the 'system' and the relatively

Figure 23. Hillside barrio (shantytown settlement) housing poor people in Caracas, Venezuela, 2007. In the brown-tech scenario, barrios around large cities continue to grow, absorbing rural migrants escaping worsening conditions for rural self-reliance due to climate change and increased corporate takeover of land for food and biofuel production.

lawless, loose but perhaps communitarian 'have–nots' with their highly flexible and nomadic subcultures living from the wastes of the 'system' and the wilds of nature. Security of the 'haves' is a constant issue, with gated communities and apartheid-style townships and barrios for the 'have-nots'. While economic depression and reduction in consumption slow greenhouse-gas emissions, the rapid expansion of strategic investment by government in new energy and urban infrastructure more than replaces the reduced private consumption, leading to a positive feedback loop that accelerates global warming.

While the elites continue to be driven by a commitment to superrationalist beliefs,[10] a sense of hollowness and lack of purpose characterises the shrinking middle class, while fundamentalist religions and cults play a stronger role in the lives of the working and unemployed classes, partly through genuine reactions to the failures of modern humanism and partly manipulated by the elites to deflect anger and disenchantment. The brown-tech scenario could be dominant and even more or less socially stable for many decades until ongoing climatic breakdown and reduced net energy return drive a shift to the lifeboats scenario.

'Top-down constriction' summarises the essence of this scenario, in that national power constricts consumption and focuses resources to maintain the nation-state in the face of deteriorating climate and reduced energy and food supply.

Green tech: distributed powerdown

Slow energy-decline rates, mild climate-change symptoms

The green-tech scenario is the most benign, in that adverse climate changes are at the low end of projections. Oil and gas production decline slowly as in the brown-tech future, so the sense of chaos and crisis is more muted, without major economic collapse or conflict. This allows resources to flow to a greater diversity of responses at the global, national, city, community and individual level. In some already densely populated poor countries, conditions worsen.

Higher commodity prices, however, allow some poorer producer economies to escape their debt cycle, while programmes to empower women result in rapid reduction in the birthrate. The gradual reduction in the capacity of countries to project power globally, owing to rising energy costs, increases national security and redirection of resources away from defence and resource capture to resource conservation and technological innovation. The consolidation of global

Figure 24. Wind turbines and wheat crop, Pommerland, Germany, 2005. In the green-tech scenario, rapid growth in renewable energy technologies continues, but the equally rapid expansion of biofuels from agricultural crops is curtailed as government policies shift from concern about fuel-supply security to food-supply security. Large-scale industrial agriculture continues to provide most nonperishable food, but high fertiliser and chemical costs accelerate the change to carbon-building organic methods.

communication systems maintains global outlooks and understandings if not global economics.

As in the brown-tech scenario, electrification is a key element in the energy transition, but the renewable energy sources of wind, biomass, solar, hydro, tidal and wave grow rapidly, developing a more diverse and distributed mix. The relatively benign climate allows a resurgence of rural and regional economies on the back of sustained and growing prices for all natural commodities, including feedstock for biofuels.

> The relatively benign climate allows a resurgence of rural and regional economies on the back of sustained and growing prices for all natural commodities, including feedstock for biofuels.

Figure 25. Organic subscription agriculture, Kyushu, Japan, 2004. In the green-tech scenario, increasing cost of fertilisers, chemicals and transportation drive a shift to more localised and urban agriculture, producing fruits, vegetables, eggs, dairy and meat products.

The principles behind organic agriculture and ecological management and resource allocation become the norm in many farming systems, helping to stabilise agriculture challenged by increasing cost of energy inputs and (albeit mild) climate change.

The accelerating conflict between biofuels and food is stabilised if not resolved by government subsidies to support food supply from agriculture, with biofuels coming mainly from forestry waste. In many regions with prime agricultural land and small populations, wealthy farmers and agribusiness corporations are the main beneficiaries, employing both high technology and cheap labour from migrant workers. In some regions, with poorer and steeper land and more diversified land ownership, smaller-scale polyculture systems designed using permaculture principles spread wealth more evenly through local communities.

Continuous contraction affects large sections of the economy, but the energy, resource and agriculture sectors along

Figure 26. Solar retrofit of an old barn at Klein Jasedow community, Pommerland, Germany, 2005. In the green-tech scenario, expansion in photovoltaic power is accelerated as new, more efficient technology becomes available, but growth is constrained by bottlenecks in production and excessive demand, so as a proportion of total energy supply solar remains small. Photo: www.kleinjasedow-familie.de

with recycling and retrofit industries experience rapid growth based on high commodity prices that are sustained despite economic recession in the main consuming economies. In some affluent countries, reform of monetary systems lowers the scale of financial collapses and refocuses capital on productive and socially useful innovation and investment.

Information technology continues to yield gains in energy and resource management, from real-time pricing and self-healing electrical grids to Internet-based ride-sharing systems and telecommuting. Conservation yields the greatest gains, with major public policies to change personal and organisational behaviour. In other countries, especially the United States, the apparent opportunities for continued economic growth, combined with government policies to support a low-carbon economy, lead to a renewable-energy investment bubble followed by a severe recession.

Figure 27. Bicycle parking at Nagora railway station, Japan, 2004. In the green-tech scenario bicycle numbers and use grow rapidly in affluent countries, leading to increased health and well-being and a radical reduction in fuel consumption.

State and city governments responsible for providing services are able to lead much of the restructuring to more compact cities and towns with increasing public-transportation infrastructure.[11] Growth in large cities (especially in coastal lowlands) is reversed by public policies ahead of the worst effects of increased energy cost and global warming, while regional cities, towns and villages see modest growth on a compact urban model that preserves prime agricultural land and develops mixed-use neighbourhoods with more local work and radically less commuting.

The placing together of many of the more optimistic aspects of energy descent may seem artificial, but there are reasons to believe that the green-tech scenario will tend toward a more egalitarian structure, with the relative shift of power from control of oil wells and mines to control of the productivity of nature via traditional land uses such as agriculture and forestry, and more novel renewable technologies.

The inherently distributed nature of these resources will

lead to more distributed economic and political power at the level of cities, with their hinterlands and organisations focused at this scale. For example, successful large-scale farmers who have reduced their dependence on energy-intensive inputs through permaculture strategies and organic methods may find new profits in more localised markets with prices sustained by policies that encourage regional self-reliance. Any profits beyond farming are likely to be invested into local energy systems that generate more employment and further reduce economic dependence on central governments and large corporations. It is possible that these same processes could lead to highly inequitable, even feudal systems. However, the universal focus on more sustainable production and reduced consumption that is not forced by remote and arbitrary central power has the tendency to foster more egalitarian responses than in the brown-tech scenario.

The substantial reductions in greenhouse-gas emissions that result from this scenario keep climate-change impacts to a minimum, thus stabilising and reinforcing the scenario's basic characteristics for at least several decades.

The success in radically reducing consumption of resources while sustaining modest growth in some local economies, combined with stabilisation of the climate, encourages a new 'sustainability' elite to consider further changes to consolidate these achievements in the face of ongoing net energy decline. The worst excesses of consumer capitalism are controlled by restriction and reform of advertising and other dysfunctional forces.

Civic culture strengthens where further transition towards a nonmaterialistic society combines with the maturation of feminism and environmentalism, and a resurgence in indigenous and traditional cultural values. These trends stabilise the accelerating loss of faith in secular humanism

Figure 28. Solar cookers, Gaia Ecovillage, Navero, Argentina, 2005. In the background are a solar hot-water heater and the thatched-roof cob community building. In the green-tech scenario, small-scale, simple, appropriate technologies begin to grow and spread, with and without government support, as part of a wider economic and political move toward relocalisation.

allowing the evolution of more spiritual 'cultures of place'. Over time, an evolution toward the Earth-steward scenario seems an obvious and natural response to the inexorable decline of nonrenewable resources. 'Distributed power-down' summarises this scenario by emphasising both the distributed nature of resources and power, and the planned contraction involved.

At their extremes the green-tech and brown-tech scenarios also describe many of the elements that could be expected in the techno-stability long-term scenario where new energy sources manage to replace fossil fuels without the stresses that lead to system-wide contraction. The current levels of ecological, economic and sociopolitical stress are the indirect indicators that we are entering the energy-descent scenarios rather than simply a transition from energetic growth to stability. Relative insulation from those stresses and the persistence of faith in the monetary accounting 'house of cards' by the upper middle class (if not the global elites) continues the confusion.[12] The lack of understanding of net energy concepts and disagreement among the experts on appropriate methods of net energy accounting, combined with political pressures from the unfolding crisis, lead to energetic descent being mistaken for 'business as usual'.

Earth steward: bottom-up rebuild

Rapid energy-decline rates, mild climate-change symptoms

In this scenario the decline in oil production after a peak in total liquids production before 2010 is at the extreme end of predictions by peak oil modellers (10-15 per cent decline per annum) and is followed by an even faster decline in gas production plus a simultaneous peak in coal production.[13] The shock to the world's fragile financial systems is overwhelming, resulting in severe economic depression and perhaps some further short, sharp resource wars.

This economic collapse and these political stresses, more than the actual shortage of resources, prevents the development of more expensive and large-scale nonrenewable resources that characterise the brown-tech scenario or the renewable resources and infrastructure of the green-tech. International and national communications networks break down.

Electricity grids become nonfunctional as cost and availability of fuels and spare parts reduce production, and lack of paying businesses and customers reduces revenues. International tensions remain, but the capacity of stronger

Figure 29. Horse-drawn bus in the town of Santi Spiritus, Cuba, 2007. The bus has modern pneumatic tyres and springs but simple wheel brakes. In the Earth-steward scenario, urban areas will be small and quiet enough that horses will again play an important role in the more limited transportation of people and goods. The ready availability of metals and modern material from salvage will create hybrids between traditional and industrial technologies.

countries to use military force is constrained by unreliable energy and parts supplies and the strong evidence that war uses more resources than it captures. Global warming is slowed dramatically and reversed by the collapse of the global consumer economy and absence of large-scale investment in new energy infrastructure.

There is a radical reduction in mass mobility of both people and goods. The food-supply chain is severely affected both on farms and through the distribution system. Energy-intensive large-scale farms supplying central marketing chains are the worst affected, leading to abandonment of even highly productive land. Shortages lead to rationing, black markets and riots for food and energy.

Increases in crime, malnutrition and disease lead to a rising death rate accelerated in some countries by epidemics and pandemics that have a major impact on social and economic capacity. The collapse in the tax base available to national and state governments reduces their power, and even city-level restructuring of infrastructure is difficult, but local govern-ment retains some degree of effective services, decision-making and possibly democracy.

Collapse of larger businesses and the difficulties in main-taining urban infrastructure leads to a hollowing out of the cities. Loss of jobs and houses leads to migration of people out of cities to smaller towns, villages and farms, with more

Figure 30. Splitting and stacking firewood for winter, Pommerland village, Germany, 2005. In the Earth-steward scenario, firewood will regain its role as the most common fuel for cooking, heating and hot water in cold and temperate climates. Reforestation will be essential in regions without forests; most reforestation will be by natural regeneration, typically of weedy exotic species on excess agricultural land that cannot be managed with limited human, animal and machine power.

robust local economies able to take advantage of the influx of labour. Impacts and demands on local soil, water and forest resources increase to severe levels in many poor countries as people move out of the cities to harvest fuel and wildlife and restart food production. In long-affluent countries, the underuse of local biological resources in the late twentieth century provides some buffer against these impacts.

Large numbers of homeless ex-urbanites form a new underclass lacking even the skills of poverty. They provide basic labour in exchange for food and accommodation on farms needing the labour. Surviving structures of power may adapt to impose a more feudal structure based on concen-

Figure 31. Volunteers and local workers hoeing weeds between corn crop, Mariza Bahia, Brazil, 2007. In the Earth-steward scenario, working together in groups becomes the norm to deal with long and arduous tasks and to maintain social connections and group security in dangerous conditions.

Figure 32. Tucano town market in semi-arid zone of rural Bahia, Brazil, 2007. With limited access to transport, weekly town markets make sense because they bring all the buyers and sellers together one day of the week. In the Earth-steward scenario, commerce is concentrated in town markets because of transportation efficiencies for people and goods.

trated control of productive farms and forests and built assets in large farming estates.

Organic and small farmers, close to markets and able to make use of labour and animal power, thrive (to the extent security allows) in a context of relatively benign and slow climate change. An explosion of home businesses based on building and equipment retrofit, maintenance and salvage starts to build a diversified economy. Further afield, biofuels from crop waste allow farmers to continue to use machinery while wood and charcoal gasification based on regrowth-forest resources near settlements and towns provide an increasing proportion of limited transportation fuel. This small-business growth in turn provides a new tax base for some form of effective local government. In some places new bioregional governments institute land reform and debt cancellation following collapse of financial institutions and central banks, allowing people to stay on their properties.

Figure 33. Small goat dairy in central Chile, 2007, an example of agricultural enterprise typical of the informal economy of Latin America that supplies local rural consumers outside of regulated and centralised industrial production. In the Earth-steward scenario, businesses of this nature provide the most formal and taxable sector of very local and simple economies.

Suburban landscapes around smaller cities and regional towns with greater social capital are transformed, with a booming and relatively egalitarian society sustained by bio-intensive/permaculture farming and retrofitting and reuse supported by resources from both the immediate rural hinterland and inner urban salvage.

This ruralisation of suburban landscape to produce food on all available open space, private and public, provides most of the fresh fruit and vegetables, dairy and small livestock products. Local currencies, food, car and fuel co-ops, and community-supported agriculture, all grow rapidly. Informal and household economies provide an increasing proportion of basic needs as corporate and government systems fail to deliver.

Around the larger cities, especially in countries where social capital and community capacity is severely eroded, most of these new developments are in gated communities providing the basic needs and security of their residents, with trade outside the community being more difficult or dangerous. Outside the gated communities salvage, fuel harvesting and animal husbandry are the main economic activities, with trade controlled by gangs and local warlords.

While the impacts on people and local environments of this scenario are severe, in previously affluent countries at least, there is also a cultural and spiritual revolution as people are released from the rat race of addictive behaviours and begin to experience the gift of resurgent community and the simple abundance of nature to provide for basic needs.

The biggest difference from the green- and brown-tech scenarios is that the rebuilding and stabilisation is no longer based on dreams of sustainability or restoring the old system. Instead people accept that each generation will have to face the challenges of further ongoing simplification and localisation of society as the fossil-resource base continues to decline. This simplification in the material domain is seen as the opportunity for growth in the spiritual domain. There is a resurgence in leadership by women and a celebration of the feminine in nature and people. 'Bottom-up rebuild' summarises this scenario by emphasising the new growth from biological and community foundations. In some ways this scenario might be considered as the archetypal one of the energy-descent future and the one in which permaculture principles and strategies are most powerfully applied.

While the impacts on people and local environments of this scenario are severe, there is also a cultural and spiritual revolution as people are released from the rat race of addictive behaviours.

Lifeboats: civilisation triage

Rapid energy-decline rates, severe climate-change

symptoms

In this scenario, supplies of high-quality fossil fuels decline rapidly, the economy fails, and human contributions to global warming collapse, but lag effects and positive feedbacks in the climate system continue to drive an acceleration of global warming. As of 2007, an increasing number of scientists believe it may already be too late to avoid catastrophic climate change.[14] In the lifeboats scenario the adverse symptoms of the brown-tech and Earth-steward scenarios combine to force a progressive collapse in most forms of economic and social organisation. Local wars, including use of nuclear weapons, accelerate collapse in some areas, but the failure of national systems of power prevents global warfare. Successive waves of famine and disease break down social and economic capacity on a larger scale than the Black Death in medieval Europe, leading to a halving of global population in a few decades.

New forms of oasis agriculture that are low-input versions of the brown-tech intensive systems evolve that stabilise food production, as chaotic seasons make traditional field agriculture and horticulture almost impossible. Forest and range-land hunting and harvesting become the predominant use of resources over large regions supporting nomadic bands. Warrior and gang cults provide meaning in a world of grief and violence, leading to the development of new religions and even languages that attempt to make sense of people's lives.

Urban areas are largely abandoned and dangerous but remain valuable as quarries for salvaging materials, especially

Figure 34. Kangaroo hunting, Australia, 2006. In the lifeboats scenario, climate change makes agriculture impossible in many marginal areas, and poverty makes livestock farming difficult (because of stock stealing). Hunting becomes the prime method for harvesting animal protein, furs and other products. Low-tech methods such as snaring and trapping are widespread, but the efficiency of firearms and their additional value as symbols of security gives status and importance to the skilled hunter and gunsmith in a world of want and fear. Powder and other components for ammunition become strategic materials.

metals. Suburban landscapes become ruralised into defensive hamlets making use of salvaged materials, urban storm water and surplus building space for mixed-household economies.

The impacts are very patchy with the worst effects in high-density, previously affluent and urbanised countries. In the most remote regions remnants of hunter-gatherer and pioneer-farmer cultures are better able to weather the changes. The relative abundance and ongoing availability of high-quality metals and other materials make a critical technological distinction from that of ancient traditional hunter-gatherer cultures.

Mountain regions, especially with surviving glacier-fed rivers, allow hydroelectric systems to be maintained and rebuilt on a smaller scale. Nutrient-rich glacier-fed rivers also sustain intensive irrigated agriculture. In some localities, especially

Figure 35. Derelict factories, Philadelphia, 2005. In the lifeboats scenario, derelict urban buildings provide salvaged material traded under difficult conditions (lack of security) to peri-urban and rural economies in exchange for food and other basic needs.

in favourable regions with accessible energy and agricultural resources, communities analogous to the monasteries of the early medieval period provide basic knowledge and skills to their surrounding communities and are thus protected by the locals from the ravages of local warlords and pirates. These communities, mostly in rural and suburban areas, and based on pre-collapse efforts of intentional communities or rich bene-factors, pursue the task of saving and condensing knowledge and cultural values for the long dark ages ahead.

'Civilisation triage' refers to the processes by which remaining social capacity (beyond meeting immediate basic needs) is focused on conserving technology and culture that could be useful to a future society, once energy descent is stabilised after a precipitous but limited collapse process.[15] This is not the dominant process of the scenario but the most significant in terms of future cultural capacity. The Christian monaster-ies that saved many of the elements of Greco-Roman culture

Figure 36. Working truck in village, Venezuela, 2007. In the lifeboats scenario, bush-mechanic skills will be valued for keeping important vehicles, machinery and tools working in the absence of spare parts and reliable fuels and lubricants.

and later provided the foundations for the Renaissance of Western civilisation is one historical example that could serve as a model for understanding how this process might work.

At its extreme, this scenario describes many of the elements of the collapse long-term future in which there is a complete breakdown in the lineage of industrial civilisation, such that future simple societies retain nothing from what we created through industrial civilisation. Drawing a distinction between this scenario and total collapse may seem pedantic, but the reasons are important. In the collapse long-term scenario, any future civilisation that could emerge learns from the lessons of ours only via archaeology and perhaps long, attenuated mythic stories. In the lifeboats scenario, the retention of cultural knowledge of the past combined with a moderately habitable environment allow new civilisations to emerge that build on at least some of the knowledge and lessons from ours.

Figure 37. Gaia Ecovillage community building, Navero, Argentina, 2007, with thatched roof, cob construction and passive solar design. In the lifeboats scenario, existing intentional communities in rural areas with shared facilities and economy may be best placed to maintain collective decision-making as well as information retention and skills training in low-tech methods of construction, food production and health maintenance.

Three factors may prevent the continuous free fall to a very low global population of hunter–gatherers.

- The first is the wild card created by the mixing of the world's biota, most notably the large numbers of tree and other species that exhibit what foresters call 'exotic vigor'.[16] This allows new recombinant ecosystems to stabilise many environments that climate scientists are now saying will become uninhabitable in extreme climate change. The release of critical minerals, most

Three factors may prevent the continuous free fall to a very low global population of hunter-gatherers.

notably phosphorus, over the last two hundred years into the biosphere may allow these new ecosystems to ultimately achieve biological productivity exceeding that possible from pre-existing systems.

• Second, the flooding of large areas of coastal lowlands complete with complex reef structures from flooded cities and infrastructure may also create the conditions for highly productive shallow waters and estuaries. These types of ecosystem are some of the most biologically productive ecosystems on the planet.[17]

Figure 38. Shaving horse used by traditional woodworker, Omaru, New Zealand, 2007. In the lifeboats scenario, traditional low-tech tool making and other skills become valued for their utility and ability to continue in the absence of industrial production.

• Third, the precipitous drop in human numbers and their
initial tendency to remain relatively aggregated to make
use of the huge resources from industrial salvage materials (and for security) should see very large regions able
to recover without harvesting and other impacts from
people.

If the knowledge of ecological processes and their creative
manipulation using minimal resources are retained and developed in the lifeboats communities, then survival and resurgence of a more-than-minimalist culture may allow global
human population to be sustained at perhaps half, rather than
one-tenth, of current levels. More importantly, it may be
possible to embed the wisdom of the lessons learned so that
unconstrained human growth does not repeat such an intense
cycle. Clearly these last thoughts are highly speculative, but
they build from the same lineage of permaculture thinking
developed over the last thirty years that informs the rest of
the scenarios.

SCENARIOS SUMMARY

The table in Figure 39 summarises the main elements and
characteristics of the four scenarios.

Scenario	Energy & Agriculture	Settlement Form & Mobility	Economy & Money	Politics	Gender	Culture & Spirituality
Brown-tech Top-down constriction	Centralised power, High-tech efficiency, Nonconvent. oil, gas, coal, nuclear, Bio-shelter agriculture	High-density cities, electric private transportation, Hinterland abandonment, Mass migration	National banks & currencies	Nationalist/ fascist, Class structure & rights, Price rationing, Population control	Male dominated & blended	Super-rationalist/ fundamental-ist dichotomy
Green-tech Distributed powerdown	Distributed network, Conservation, gas, wind, solar, forest, organic agriculture	Compact towns and small cities, electric public transportation, Telecommuting	Regional currencies & funds	City state & hinterland, Markets/ rationing, Democracy	Balanced & blended	Humanist/ Eco-rationalist
Earth steward Bottom-up rebuild	Distributed local hydro, methane, Industrial salvage, Forest, organic & garden agriculture	Ruralisation of suburbia, rural resettlement, minimal mobility	Local currency, barter	Town and bioregion, Participatory democracy? Neo-feudalism	Female dominated & gendered	Earth spirituality
Lifeboats Civilisation triage	Distributed local, Forest, range-land, Industrial salvage, Oasis Agriculture	Hamlet and gated communities, nomads	Household & barter, precious metals	Feudal system, Patriarchal authority	Male dominated & gendered	Warrior cult

Figure 39. Summary of the four climate-change and energy-descent scenarios in terms of key characteristics that can be used to make comparisons with the previous and currently waning characteristics of globalised industrial systems.

INTERPRETING THE SCENARIOS

GLOBAL AND LOCAL PERSPECTIVES

THE SCENARIOS AS described are biased towards look-
ing at the future for the billion or so relatively affluent persons
who primarily live in the long-industrialised nations, mostly
of Europe and North America but including Japan, Australia
and New Zealand. For many people outside these countries
the promise of benefits from global industrial culture are just
that – promises. The general history tells of local and self-
reliant economies and communities decaying or collapsing
as they are displaced by monetary economies and media and
consumer ideologies. This is a process often associated with
migration from rural to urban areas. The debate about the
balance of benefits and disadvantages from these changes has
been intense for thirty years.[1]

Very few proponents or even critics of conventional
economic development are yet considering energy-descent
scenarios, or the increased vulnerabilities to them that result
from this loss of self-reliance. Poor people crowded into
barrios around supercities completely dependent on meagre
cash flows to maintain access to food and fuel are less able to
provide for themselves when these systems fail. Five months
in Latin America has given me cause to think deeply about
these vulnerabilities that are already unfolding in many places
where, compared to wages, fuel prices are ten times more
than they are in Australia.

On the other hand, one cannot experience life in many

poorer countries without also considering how recent the changes have been. In many places people still know how to grow food and in some cases can return to their home villages as soon as economic conditions suggest this will be more rewarding (even if it is only to labour on a relative's farm) than hustling in the city for a dollar. Even when this is not possible, the sense of how resourceful and flexible people can be in what we might think of as extreme conditions is a strength.

It is not just the ability to cope with deprivation but more the psychosocial capacity to accept life as it happens without the fixed expectation that leads to inevitable disappointment. While teaching a course in Mexico I was summarising the energy-descent scenarios session with reference to the house fire-insurance analogy; that it was not necessary to believe your house would burn down to have fire insurance. The mostly middle-class Mexicans laughed at my analogy because most Mexican homeowners don't have fire insurance. It is this easy-going acceptance of life that may be one of the characteristics that enables Mexicans to weather the storms that are surely coming.

On the other hand, in Australia and other long-affluent countries, many generations of steadily growing affluence and high expectations have created a psychological and social brittleness that suggests we may not weather the storms as well as we should. As a teenager I came to the conclusion that Australia was vulnerable to the attractions of fascism if and when social and economic conditions become much tougher. This early insight provided a foundation for the brown-tech scenario.

In some nations, economic collapse and sustained conflict over the last few decades have simulated some aspects of energy descent. Most of the evidence is not good, with break-down of law and order, food insecurity, falling life expectancy

and mass migration. Russia, Argentina, Cuba, Zimbabwe and
North Korea are examples of relatively affluent and industrialised countries that have experienced sustained conditions
analogous to those possible from more general and global
energy descent. An increasing amount of research and analysis
within the peak-oil network has focused on these countries
to gain greater understanding of the hazards and opportunities of energy-descent futures.[2] Most notable is the Cuban
experience, which is remarkably positive and has provided a
great boost to permaculture and other activists trying to show
the opportunities from energy descent.

CUBA: BROWN TECH, GREEN TECH OR EARTH STEWARD?

During the crisis of the 'Special Period' in Cuba in the
early 1990s the power of strong central government did not
weaken, let alone fail. In some ways the government led by
Fidel Castro represents many of the elements of the brown-
tech world. On the other hand, Cuba is not a very large
country and can be considered as one bioregion with Havana
as its capital, so the scale of governance is more akin to that
proposed for the green-tech scenario. Further, many of the
strategies for coping with the crisis from urban agriculture
to bicycle and public transportation are emblematic of the
green-tech scenario.[3] Health and education statistics for Cuba
also rule out the more severe conditions associated with Earth
steward, let alone lifeboats. However, while in Cuba in 2007
I became aware of some aspects of the crisis that did give
insight into likely conditions in the more extreme scenarios.

During two trips in the countryside I observed extensive
growth of marabou (*Dichrostachys cinerea*, a spiny leguminous

shrub) over large areas that appeared to have been farmland. The rapid spread of marabou occurred during the crisis, and today it covers about 20 per cent of the farmland.[4] This and similar species were previously common in the landscape, mostly as a component of living fences and hedges. When the crisis hit, supplies of grains to feed the industrialised dairy industry collapsed, and many of the dairy cows died in the dry season.

My hypothesis is that prior to dying, the cows would have eaten the dry pastures to bare ground and the living fences to sticks.[5] The seeds of the marabou consumed by the cows pass through in manure, so in the succeeding wet season a complete crop of thorn shrubs would have emerged and dominated the recovering pastures. Despite the desperate need for food, the absence of fuel to plough the land for crops or to resow pastures allowed the shrubs to take over the land. This example illustrates how valuable resources such as farmland can lie idle in the face of desperate need.

The process of recovering the land from the thicket forests is a slow one even with better economic conditions, but it has also produced benefits that are slow to be recognised. Increased carbon sequestration has been substantial and plant diversity and wildlife is increasing as the shrubs mature. The soil-rejuvenating characteristics of these spiny legume shrubs may be building an asset that will be more valuable to Cuba as global energy descent begins to have an impact. Two low-energy pathways to more productive and sustainable use of the land are possible. One is to use goats to reclaim the land as pasture.[6] Alternatively, accelerated succession to mixed-food forest by selective seeding and planting could create agro-forestry systems that continue to increase woody biomass and food production both from fruit and nuts.

It is significant that both of these changes would require

further changes in Cuban eating habits. This is connected to another sobering impression, in the otherwise quite positive picture, that Cubans remained reluctant to change their traditional food habits even during the crisis and mostly have gone back to those habits after the crisis. The fact that a diet with less meat and dairy and a greater diversity of tropical vegetables, fruits and nuts could be more easily and sustainably produced will require continued efforts on many fronts and/or a longer cycle of deprivation to shift the deeply entrenched European food-culture heritage in this tropical country.

Perhaps more relevant to countries with less government controls over the economy, Argentina provides some interesting examples of revitalisation of local economies as central currencies and economies broke down, although most of these stopped once the monetary economy was re-established.[7]

One of the uncertainties that emerges from reflecting on these examples of economic contraction is how different the situation will be when the dominant economic powers experience these problems. The instabilities and weakening of a globalised economic system will reduce the capacity to project power. Consequently we can expect conditions in local bioregions and nations increasingly to reflect the local resources, economy and culture and be less driven by remote and global forces. As always, this will precipitate new threats but also opportunities.

DEPRESSING AND POSITIVE SCENARIOS

Another reaction to the scenarios by some participants in courses is that the brown-tech scenario seems a depressing but realistic assessment of the situation in many affluent countries, while the green-tech scenario looks more utopian and unrealistic, but one that could almost be 'sold' as a desirable future by Green parties of Western democracies.[8]

The argument that the distributed power provided by resurgent rural economies will ameliorate the centralised and inequitable structures that lead to the brown-tech world may be seen as a weak one, especially for people who are suspicious of the concept that energy and resources are what fundamentally drive economic, social and political systems. Similarly the relative positive nature of Earth steward compared with lifeboats is partly predicated on the distributed rather than concentrated nature of resources and wealth (and of course the gift of a relatively benign climate).

It is possible to see some good and bad potentials (depending in part on our philosophical bent) in all four scenarios. Perhaps as an act of faith in human values and maturity, I believe we can better shape our responses to each of the scenarios if as individuals and as communities and nations we recognise the constraining forces that are beyond our control. We can then consider how basic human values and needs can be sustained without wasting resources on projects or objectives that may have little chance of altering the fundamental dynamics of our world.

Of course this reaction can be seen as negative, defeatist or even contributing to the realisation of these undesirable scenarios. In the ad hoc Internet community of peak-oil activism that has sprung up the last few years, the divide between the 'doomers' and the 'optimists' has been a notable one. Since 2005 the worsening evidence on climate change has led to more of the experts in that field moving toward a 'doomer' perspective on the climate front. Part of the process of moving beyond this simplistic and mostly counterproductive debate is to see some of the positive potentials that exist in energy-descent scenarios.

Permaculture activism has a long history of being informed by a negative view of the state of the world. But these perspectives drive an optimistic, opportunity-based response that can empower people to creative action and adaptation in the face of adversity. The fact that permaculture activists privately and even publicly look forward to some aspects of these scenarios may be seen by some as naïve or even immoral. On the other hand, an increasing number of people around the world find permaculture an empowering focus for ethical and practical action.

My recent experience from presenting the energy-descent scenarios in Australia, New Zealand, Brazil, Cuba, Mexico and Argentina in permaculture courses as well as other gatherings of sustainability professionals is that they can be very empowering, although I recognise the risk that they still pose in triggering denial or depression and paralysis.

DIFFERENT SCENARIOS
IN DIFFERENT PLACES

Australia and New Zealand provide examples of two very similar affluent countries in the South Pacific that may already be on very different trajectories and that reflect the dynamics of these scenarios. As the previous prime minister John Howard proclaimed, Australia is one of the new energy superpowers. This claim is supported by the fact that Australia is the largest global exporter of coal, one of the largest exporters of gas with the seventh largest reserves, and has the largest reserves of uranium as well as many other minerals. On the other hand, climate change modelling suggests Australia is perhaps the most vulnerable of OECD countries, a vulnerability highlighted by the recent and continuing

drought. These are the essential conditions for the emergence
of brown-tech. The 'debate' about nuclear power initiated by
the previous Australian government and the rush to build
desalination plants and super-pipelines to address the water
crisis are emblematic of this trend. The change of federal
government to the Labour Party is likely to further concen-
trate power at the federal level and could lead to a more rapid
abandonment of free-market capitalism, further entrenching
the brown-tech scenario.[9]

New Zealand, on the other hand, has very little in the way
of minable energy and resources, but, relative to its population, it has extremely rich biophysical resources to support
agriculture, forestry and renewable energies. The local impacts
of climate change are predicted to be much less severe, allowing New Zealand to take advantage of these distributed rural
resources. New Zealand thus looks like a strong candidate
for green tech. Without going into a detailed analysis of the
emerging trends in the Australian and New Zealand economies and politics, it is sufficient to say Australia and New
Zealand have been diverging for some time. This suggests that
these underlying differences between the energy and resource
bases of these two countries may have been contributing to
the emerging differences at the political and even the social
levels.

STEPPED ENERGY-DESCENT PATHWAYS
LINKING THE SCENARIOS

As previously mentioned, energy descent may not be a
continuous gradual process. Instead it could be characterised
by an initial crisis that sets the conditions for a new order that
is stable for some time before another crisis leads to further

descent. The growth of energy and resultant technological complexity over the last two hundred years has involved
varying rates of change, plateaus and even regressions during
wars and depressions, but energy descent is likely to be much
more variable than energy ascent. This is consistent with our
commonsense understanding that growth is a more consistent
process than decline.

Natural ecosystems tend to maintain homeostasis under
stress through the allocation of stored resources. If the conditions continue to deteriorate, then further stress can fracture
the homeostasis. If the stress involves a reduction in energy
availability, the system may collapse. But total collapse and
system disintegration is rare, at least in the short term. More
typically a restabilisation occurs at a lower level of energy
processing and organisational complexity. The new homeostasis will typically be stable for some time before declining
energy availability precipitates another crisis. This may also
be a model for how human societies respond to the crisis of
resource and energy decline. It also makes sense that natural disasters, or a crisis such as war, rarely continue for very
long but they shape the new state that emerges in their aftermath. If crisis does persist at an intense level for years then
psychosocial systems reorganise around the crisis as the new
normality.

The graph in Figure 40 shows these two pathways from
Hubbert's peak of oil (and net energy production). The
discontinuities are periods of extreme crisis, conflict and/or
breakdown. Each scenario represents a homeostasis that tends
to be self-maintaining until further stress precipitates a further
unravelling.

The red pathway in the graph is more extreme, and
after continued growth leads to a precipitous drop through
natural disasters, economic depression and/or war. Brown

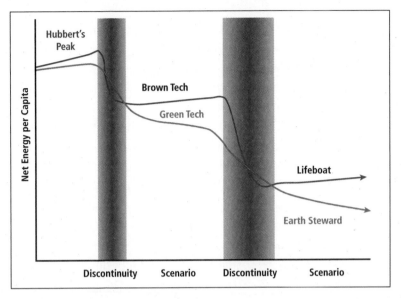

Figure 40. Stepped energy-descent pathways.

tech emerges as the new world order, allowing recovery and modest growth before further natural disasters or climate change and resource depletion precipitate another discontinuity, leading to a lifeboats world. The green pathway is less extreme, with a lower peak and a gentler decline through the first discontinuity to the green-tech scenario, while the descent to Earth steward is even more continuous, driven by ongoing depletion and decay of infrastructure from the Hubbert's peak and green-tech worlds.

The chart also shows the relative levels of net energy availability per capita. This is much more speculative than the general concept of the stepwise descent or the relationships among the scenarios, because it depends on many variables. I've shown the brown-tech and lifeboats scenarios as processing more net energy per capita than the green-tech and Earth-steward scenarios, respectively. A range of factors contributes to this speculative maths, and hides some harsh

realities. Depending on how net energy is understood and
evaluated, a higher total energy base in brown tech may
maintain greater organisational and technological complexity,
but green tech may be more energetically efficient at providing real human services.

A harsher discontinuity leading to brown tech may produce
a higher death rate in the more urbanised populations, while
more severe controls on births may further reduce populations. The numbers of people the energy base needs to
support strongly affects the per capita level, so a higher per
capita figure may reflect lower birthrates and/or higher death
rates rather than a more energy-rich society. Alternatively, the
lower death rate during the gentler discontinuity leading to
green tech combined with a higher birthrate to tap the more
distributed rural resources of the green-tech world may result
in overall higher populations. Although net energy per capita
is lower, life may on average be better than in the brown-tech
scenario.

Similarly, in the second discontinuity crisis the death rate
increases but more so in the red pathway to lifeboats. The
lack of community capacity in the midst of massive material-
salvage opportunities combines with the lower population
to deliver relatively high net energy per capita even though
life is very harsh. The more abundant distributed renewable
resources of the Earth-steward scenario leads to a higher
birthrate (to tap those resources). Combined with the lower
death rate, the higher overall population gives a very low net
energy per capita. Efficient communitarian economies and
a spiritual rather than material culture may make for higher
levels of well-being despite limited resources per person.

NESTED SCENARIOS

Yet another way to consider these scenarios is to see them as all emerging simultaneously, one nested within the other. Figure 41 shows the scenarios nested with their associated organisational and energetic scale, from the distributed and human scale of households to the centralised power and scale of government and corporations. This suggests that the four organisational levels represented by the scenarios from the household to the national level will all be transformed as global systems weaken and contract, but none will fail completely. In a sense this is implicit in each scenario in any case and resolves the difficulty in imagining the Earth-steward and lifeboats scenarios with a complete absence of city- and national-level power structures, even if their functions and influence are very weak or attenuated by being away from the centres of power.

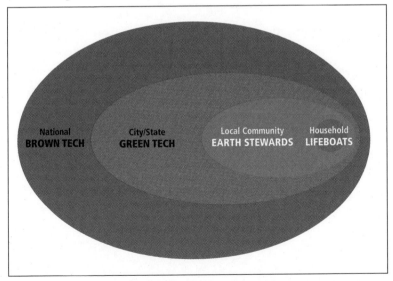

Figure 41. Energy-descent scenarios nested by scale of most relevant level of organisation.

In explaining this concept of nested scenarios in the aforementioned course in Mexico, I suggested that in the Earth-steward and lifeboats scenarios there could still be a government in Mexico City issuing edicts, but that no one, outside the much reduced city, would hear or take any notice. Like the reaction to my insurance example, my Mexican students laughed and suggested that no one took any notice of the government in Mexico City now. This humorous response actually reflects an ongoing process of fragmentation in Mexico, where autonomous movements in some regions and drug lords in others already rival the central and state governments in the provision of security, extraction of taxes and provision of services.

The other reason for considering that aspects of all scenarios will simultaneously emerge in all regions is the structural commitment of each level of governance to systems that can work at their respective levels. It is natural for national governments and large corporations to implement the systems that characterise the brown-tech scenario because these systems are commensurate with the organisational scale in which they work. Similarly, it is natural for city and bioregional (state) governments to implement the somewhat more distributed, diverse and smaller-scale systems of the green-tech scenario. Middle-sized businesses using regional resources and serving regional markets will naturally work to reinforce this scenario.

Following this logic we can see that smaller forms of organisation (small business and local government) could manage many of the strategies applicable to the Earth-steward scenario

It is natural for national governments and large corporations to implement the systems that characterise the brown-tech scenario.

> Any planning for lifeboats is mostly a private activity of people who lack total faith in the stability of our economy and society.

while the household or closed community is the natural level of organisation to contemplate the lifeboats scenario. This nested hierarchy of scenarios explains why any planning for lifeboats is mostly a private activity of people who lack total faith in the stability of our economy and society. Similarly, many community activists work toward strategies that level the playing field and develop communitarian cultures, and would be potent in an Earth-steward world, just as earnest middle-level managers and planners work toward the green-tech world as the best progressive evolution from what we have. Many of the elite 'movers and shakers', often from long-established wealthy families in affluent countries and who move between the upper levels of corporations, governments and global governance organisations, believe the brown-tech world is the hard reality that must be worked with (although this can hardly be acknowledged publicly).[10]

I think the nested concept is one of the most insightful and empowering ways to think about these scenarios, because it helps us understand the apparent contradictions between different perspectives and motivations of different groups in society and even contradiction within our own thoughts and behaviours. For example, it is common for people to have private thoughts about the lifeboats or perhaps Earth-steward futures, while most of people's public behaviour as workers and consumers reinforces brown tech or perhaps green tech. The private thoughts are often internally critiqued as antisocial or at least naïve, while the public actions are often internally critiqued as driven by powerful outside forces. This nested model can help us better integrate these different aspects of ourselves.

RELEVANCE OF MAINSTREAM IDEAS OF SUSTAINABILITY TO ENERGY DESCENT

Mainstream approaches to sustainability tend to assume stability if not expansion in the energy flows available to humanity, even if there are major transitions in the nature of the energy sources. Consequently, continuity of many of the structures underpinning current social and economic systems is assumed.

For example, modern affluent urban life in a society dominated by service economies may be transformed by revolutions in efficiency but will remain the norm for future sustainable society. Further, it is widely assumed that food production and management of biological resources to provide for human needs will remain a minor part of future economies, and that geopolitical stability will allow globalised trade and other global governance regimes to become increasingly effective as instruments to establish sustainable systems.

These are not so different from the 'business as usual' assumptions about constant growth, but they require not only Herculean efforts to build a new energy infrastructure before energy becomes too expensive and unreliable, but also massive reductions in our greenhouse-gas emissions today, if not yesterday.

There is also the small problem of reforming the monetary system away from dependence on perpetual growth without inducing financial collapse. I say 'small problem' ironically, of course, because growth in economic activity is essential to support the debt-based currency that is the very foundation of our money and banking system stretching back to the beginnings of capitalism and its economic precursors.

For these reasons I feel the techno-stability long-term future has even fewer prospects than the default future of techno-explosion. Maybe this also helps explain the deep resistance and antagonism in the centres of political and economic power to questioning of the logic of growth. Whether it comes from an ecological or sociological perspective, questioning economic growth threatens the very basis of our economic system. The lip service to environmental sustainability (so long as it can maintain essential growth) reflects this understanding.

> The economic hardliners could be right: there is no way to stop the train of global industrial capitalism (other than by crashing).

Consequently, more idealistic notions of steady-state green economics are automatically rejected as 'throwing the baby out with the bathwater'. While I have been as critical of the concept of continuous economic growth as most environmentalists and scientists, I also recognise that attempts to avoid the ecological precipice by reducing economic growth could bring down the whole system, just as Gorbachev's glasnost contributed to the unravelling of the Soviet system. The economic hardliners could be right: there is no way to stop the train of global industrial capitalism (other than by crashing).

Despite these doubts about the logic behind many mainstream approaches to sustainability, they have contributed greatly in spreading new environmental thinking and many of the practical strategies that appear to be moving in the right direction. For example, the Natural Step concept aims to protect biophysical systems by creating closed-loop industrial manufacturing through continual improvements in performance.[11] It has been very influential in Scandinavia and has been adopted by some of the more progressive manufacturing corporations. Rapidly rising costs of energy and commodities will reinforce many of the Natural Step strategies, but it will also increase the costs of adopting some of the more elaborate environmental technologies that have been used to ensure there is no contamination of natural or human environments.

Natural Step might work to some degree in the green-tech world but would seem futile in the brown-tech, technically and organisationally impractical in the Earth-steward, and meaningless in the lifeboats. The vast majority of concepts and strategies to reduce greenhouse-gas emissions could be similarly analysed as having uncertain relevance at best to energy-descent scenarios.

The table in Figure 42 quantifies my view that mainstream approaches to sustainability have quite low relevance to energy-descent scenarios. Low scores do not mean that these

MAINSTREAM CONCEPTS		
Scenario	Typical Strategies	Fundamental Principles
Green Tech	★★☆☆☆	★★★☆☆
Brown Tech	★☆☆☆☆	★★☆☆☆
Earth Steward	☆☆☆☆☆	★☆☆☆☆
Lifeboats	☆☆☆☆☆	☆☆☆☆☆
Totals	3/16	6/16

Figure 42. Relevance of mainstream concepts of sustainability to energy-descent scenarios; scoring both current strategies and underlying principles against each scenario.

ideas will completely disappear but that they will tend to shift from their current status as the innovative and influential cutting edge of the economy to reflecting a past era – rather than their objective of becoming the norm within a sustainable society. The table also shows that, in general, fundamental principles will have more utility than specific strategies and technologies that are currently being applied as good examples of these concepts.

RELEVANCE OF ENVIRONMENTAL PRINCIPLES

Renewable energy sources

A good example of the likely greater relevance of environmental principles when compared with specific strategies and technologies can be seen in relation to future energy sources. In fossil-fuelled global industrial systems, energy supply has been generally concentrated in a few big powerful sources. A common principle in sustainability thinking is that a greater diversity of smaller and more distributed power sources will replace current fossil fuel, large hydro and nuclear sources. The current rollout of wind power and, to a lesser extent, solar electric as future technologies illustrates this general principle, and both are widely recognised as central to the techno-stability future. But energy descent may see growth in these particular energy sources slow or fail while older distributed sources such as wood and small-scale hydro could grow rapidly. In a rapidly changing world appropriate design principles provide more guidance than specific strategies and technologies.

Biodiversity in natural-resource management

In the field of natural-resource management the general principle of valuing biodiversity is likely to persist to some degree, at least in the green-tech world, but the examples of vegetation management exclusively focused on local indigenous species, which are common today, will seem very dated as reflecting a world of rising wealth and constant climate.[12]

Arguably, the principle of valuing biodiversity may even grow in strength as the current economic drivers favouring monoculture in agriculture and forestry weaken and are overtaken by viral forms of polyculture better able to use soil and water resources without inputs, and better able to serve mixed local markets. This process will allow the principle of valuing biodiversity to spread from the relative 'cultural ghetto' of conservation management in affluent countries to a more powerful expression of the permaculture version of the principle of 'use and value diversity'. This very change may be experienced by those wedded to the current dominant views within the field of conservation biology as heresy to be resisted. This is just one example of how energy-descent scenarios will challenge some cherished beliefs within the environmental movement, while making others natural and obvious. Energy descent demands that we consider more radical approaches to achieving environmental and social objectives.

META-SCENARIOS OF PERMACULTURE

Permaculture as an environmental design concept with a long and evolving lineage of action around the world provides one such framework for developing new and reinforcing existing strategies that should be adaptive in energy-descent scenarios.

In *Permaculture: Principles and Pathways Beyond Sustainability* I explain the importance of design principles as the basis for generating new strategies and techniques in a world of change and uncertainty. The table in Figure 43 shows how permaculture (especially when it is understood through its design principles) more so than currently applied strategies has a closer fit with energy-descent scenarios than many other sustainability concepts that have achieved more mainstream acceptance in affluent countries. While the numerical scores for permaculture compared with those for mainstream sustainability can be taken with a grain of salt, the broad thrust is clear.

This table may reflect a claim of permaculture's central relevance to energy descent, but it also suggests an equal challenge to permaculture educators, activists and designers to use design principles more effectively to identify strategies, techniques and working models that are tuned to emerging rather than past conditions.[13]

Each scenario presents quite different opportunities and challenges, including ethical dilemmas for permaculture and related environmental and social activists. The analysis of the

PERMACULTURE CONCEPTS		
Scenario	Typical Strategies	Fundamental Principles
Green Tech	★★☆☆	★★★☆
Brown Tech	★☆☆☆	★★★☆
Earth Steward	★★★☆	★★★★
Lifeboats	★★☆☆	★★★☆
Totals	8/16	13/16

Figure 43. Relevance of permaculture to energy-descent scenarios; scoring both typical permaculture strategies and design principles against each scenario.

Each scenario presents quite different opportunities and challenges, including ethical dilemmas for permaculture and related environmental and social activists.

relevance of permaculture to the energy-descent scenarios makes it possible to imagine meta-scenarios of how permaculture and related activism might influence society in ways different from those of today. Clearly these meta-scenarios are even more speculative than the energy-descent scenarios, but they do provide a stimulus, especially for young people to imagine themselves in the energy-descent future.

I imagine that permaculture *(by principle and model, if not in name) will become the dominant p*aradigm in the Earth-steward scenario. Those with a long track record of achievement will become the natural leaders within new emergent power structures, primarily at the local level, that will be more effective than higher levels of governance and organisation. The ethical and design challenges will be those associated with leadership and power. Because 'power' at this (and all levels) will be very weak, it will be characterised more by inspiration and wise council than the capacity to make binding decisions. Transparent and collaborative leadership that draws from the whole community, accepts slow evolutionary change and avoids the imposition of ideology is likely to be most effective in conserving resources and continuing to build a nature-based culture.

Permaculture is also highly relevant to survival in the life-boats scenario. The focus on provision of basic needs first and maintenance of seed and other genetic resources and skills to salvage and 'make do' will all be essential. Those with considerable knowledge, skills and ability to provide for others, as

well as those who have good communication and organisation skills in difficult conditions, are likely to become natural
leaders of lifeboats households and communities. The ethical
and design challenges are not so much those of broader and
collaborative leadership, but more likely will be those represented by having to decide whom to let into the lifeboats
without threatening the survival of those already on board.
The ability to integrate and defend the group without senti-
mentality while providing for the community and maintaining knowledge critical to long-term cultural survival is the
task of those able to think beyond everyday survival.

In the green-tech scenario 'sustainability' becomes the dominant paradigm of more localised city and bioregional governance structures. Permaculture and related concepts have high
status and receive resources from government and businesses
to help further develop local food production and community
economies that can buffer against further energy and ecological crises. For the permaculture activist this is a more familiar
condition where there is ongoing, even rapid, growth in influence, but where the dominant paradigm is still focused in the
economic and technological domains rather than the ecological domain as the source of wealth and meaning.

The primary ethical dilemma is that of comfortable
co-option by the new sustainability elites, in the context of
their heroic successes in avoiding the worst impacts of energy
descent. Should permaculture activists quietly accept the
status and resources that flow from these sustainability elites
and focus on the slow change of society through practical
works, or should they criticise the new elite for not accepting
that energy descent will precipitate further crises unless we
localise and simplify our economies further? The ability to
lead by example and provide clear and persuasive articulation
of values and goals beyond the prevailing mainstream leads

> The challenges for permaculture activists
> are somewhat analogous to those working in
> some poorer countries today: trying to assist
> the disadvantaged with simple technologies
> and solutions while avoiding threats from
> repressive central power.

to progressively more influence as the ongoing realities of energy descent unfold.

In the brown-tech scenario, permaculture remains marginal to the mainstream, although it provides hope and some solutions for the increasing numbers of disenfranchised and alienated who reject, or are rejected by, the systems controlled by powerful central governments. The challenges for permaculture activists are somewhat analogous to those working in some poorer countries today: trying to assist the disadvantaged with simple technologies and solutions while avoiding threats from repressive central power.

Too much structure, organisation and prominence could see such activism ruthlessly crushed as a threat to the system. Anarchistic and invisible modes of activism are likely to be more effective. Of course there are also those attempting to use ethical and design principles to reform the system from within (with all the attendant contradictions). Quiet and persistent collaboration between these two levels of activism could see a graceful descent to Earth stewardship, while failure could lead to the lifeboats as the last option for the salvage of civilisation.

CONCLUSION

THIS EXPLORATION OF energy-descent scenarios has been an organic one that began with a didactic intention to highlight how large-scale energetic and environmental factors shape history more than ideologies and the heroic actions of individuals. But my purpose was to empower those committed to ecological values and social justice to be effective in their quest to create the world we want, rather than just resist the world we don't want. Finally it has become about telling a story that can help bring that world to life, an apparent contradiction to the premise I began with. Although the primary lesson about the large-scale forces that control the course of history may be true for the long periods of stability, during periods of ecological and cultural chaos small groups of people have been instrumental in those transitions.

In nature, disturbance events (such as fire, flood or drought) or eruptive disturbances from within an ecosystem, such as insect plagues or fungal disease, are often understood as examples of system dysfunction. Alternatively, they can be understood as either initiating another succession cycle that brings renewed life or a novel force that deflects the ecosystem in different directions determined by the chance arrival of new species or other factors. The ecosystems that emerge from these periods of disturbance can be quite different from those that preceded them, and these changes can be characterised from a systems ecology perspective as either degradation of biophysical resources and productivity, and/or ones involving new evolutionary pathways. The lesson from nature is that evolution of life works in strange ways that cannot be fully predicted.

The historian William Irwin Thompson's interpretation of the creation of the world's 'first university' by Pythagoras suggests similar processes at work when civilisation finds itself in a cultural dead end or design cul-de-sac.[1] Pythagoras had been an initiate of the Egyptian mystery schools that were part of a decaying theocracy in the sixth century BC. Pythagoras and his followers secularised some of the hidden and arcane knowledge, but his school in Calabria was burnt to the ground in some local political dispute. Pythagoras died a broken man, but his followers fled to Greece where they found fertile social conditions for their ideas and values. This was the beginning of the flowering of classical Grecian culture that we recognise as the origins of Western civilisation. In a similar story Thompson describes how the penniless monks of Lindisfarne converted the British Isles to Christianity in the sixth century AD. They had no power, but their spiritual message, shaped to reflect Celtic traditions, was transformative in a country in the aftermath of the collapse of the Roman Empire and where no one any longer knew the function of Stonehenge. For a couple of generations a form of free, anarchic Christianity provided spiritual meaning, but the Vikings burnt the monastery to the ground.

Like Pythagoras and the monks of Lindisfarne we live in a world of collapsing culture where we have to choose what is worthwhile at this great turning point in history. We are faced with the mixed pieces of myriad broken traditional cultures of the world and the novel and shining bits of unravelling industrial modernity. All of this will end in the dustbin of history. Our task is to choose which pieces of these jigsaw puzzles will be useful in creating an energy-descent culture, the boundaries, features and colours of which we can scarcely imagine. What is worth saving? What are the limits of our capacity? We have little time to decide and act. We must commit to concrete actions and projects. We must stake our claim, not for ourselves but for the future. In committing to our task we should remember the stories of Pythagoras and the monks of Lindisfarne. It is not the project but the living process that will be the measure of our actions.

Let us act as if we are part of nature's striving for the next evolutionary way to respond creatively to the recurring cycles of energy ascent and descent that characterise human history and the more ancient history of Gaia, the living planet. Imagine that our descendants and our ancestors are watching us.

NOTES

Chapter 1

1. Daniel Yergin's The Prize: The Epic Quest for Oil, Money, and Power
    (New York: Simon & Schuster, 1991) is often quoted as the 'definitive
    history' of oil and its role in shaping the twentieth century. It certainly
    corrects ignorance on the importance of energy. With the perspective of
    almost two decades' hindsight, however, it is easier to see the author's bias
    in portraying the power plays of the West as protecting national interest
    while those of competing powers and ideologies as being marked by evil,
    greed and stupidity. See the review by Derrick Jensen www
    .amazon.com/review/R2YYOUX9S8BPC4/ref=cm_cr_pr
    _viewpnt#R2YYOUX9S8BPC4.

    Yergin's focus on the technology and politics of oil, by reinforcing
    the orthodoxy of the 1980s and 1990s that resource limits were not
    a concern, also laid the foundations for the currently widespread and
    dangerous view that current supply restrictions are due to 'above-ground
    factors' rather than geological limits of peak oil.

    For a recent and up-to-date overview of oil history from a leftist
    perspective see Michael P. Byron, *Infinity's Rainbow: The Politics of Energy,
    Climate and Globalisation* (New York: Algora Publishing, 2006). For a very
    humorous but informative introduction to the history of oil (including
    the Iraqi invasion and peak oil), see Robert Newman, *A Short History of
    Oil* (downloadable from Google Video).

2. This faith derives from European Enlightenment thinking.

3. In 1950 Sir Earnest Titterton, the chief advisor to the Australian
    government on nuclear power at the time, asserted that by 1980 nuclear
    power would be too cheap to bother metering the use.

4. For example, cheap energy allowed energy-dense plastic, aluminum, steel
    and concrete to replace wood in the building industry, thus depressing
    the demand and price for wood and the value of forests. Similarly, fossil-
    fuel-based fabrics reduced the demand for cotton and wool, depressing
    their price with flow-on effects to all agricultural commodities. The
    Green Revolution increased grain production by increased use of energy-
    dense fertilisers and pesticides. This in turn increased food surpluses and
    depressed prices.

Chapter 2

1. Since 2001 many of the positions of established players in the global economy, including corporations, governments and multilateral institutions, have constantly shifted. This could be interpreted as open and flexible response to new evidence, or, more cynically, as defensive repositioning to protect established interests for as long as possible from public awareness of the problems. This process in relation to climate change is now widely understood.

   Ironically the evidence for the approximate timing of peak oil was around for decades before the evidence for climate change, so the potential for misleading the public (and the intelligentsia) by those with the best information about global oil production and reserves is greater.

2. Some, such as Joseph Tainter, *The Collapse of Complex Societies* (Cambridge: Cambridge University Press, 1988), and Jared Diamond, *Collapse: How Societies Choose to Fail or Succeed* (New York: Viking, 2005) use the term *collapse* to describe any ongoing reduction in complexity of the organisation of civilisations. While their work is of great importance, I want to draw a distinction between what I mean by *collapse* as the sudden failure and loss of most of the organisational complexity (such that succeeding generations retain little use or even memory of such systems) and *descent* as a progressive if erratic process where the loss of complexity is gradual and succeeding generations have some awareness of, and knowledge from, that peak of complexity.

3. From advice to governments that nuclear power would be too cheap to bother metering to children's magazines promising holidays to Mars, the hubris about the techno-explosion in the boom era of the 1950s and 1960s was exceptional.

4. By *social capacity* I mean the informal processes of mutual support and conflict resolution that allow communities to provide education, welfare, insurance and other functions, with or without support from the formal structures of government. The level of volunteerism is one widely recognised measure of social capacity, but even this measure captures only the more formal end of social capacity, which mostly works as a by-product of very ordinary interactions between citizens.

5. The concept of *emergy accounting* as developed by Howard T. Odum provides a systematic and quantitative synthesis of how these forms of wealth combine, with more basic energy and resources, to drive human systems.

6. See William R. Catton, *Overshoot: The Ecological Basis of Revolutionary Change* (Urbana, IL: University of Illinois Press, 1980).

7. Clearly, by pinning the relevance of permaculture to an energy-descent future, I may contribute to the current perception of its marginal relevance to a world of energy growth. But on balance I believe this transparency about our own assumptions and biases is a strength rather than a weakness. In this way we acknowledge ourselves as activists rather than simply observers.

8. See article by John Michael Greer at the Energy Bulletin Website, www. energybulletin.net/20157.html.

9. See 'Downshifting in Australia' (pdf) (The Australia Institute, 2003), suggesting that 'downshifters' moving to a lower-consuming, more satisfying lifestyle make up as much as 23 per cent of the Australian population.

10. The transition towns process in Britain, initiated by permaculture activist Rob Hopkins, is an excellent example of this positive community response to the realities coming from peak oil and climate change. See Hopkins' *The Transition Handbook: From Oil Dependency to Local Resilience* (Totnes, Devon: Green Books, 2008), an invaluable resource for this positive change process.

11. For example, Australian sociologist Ted Trainer's *The Simpler Way: Working for Transition from a Consumer Society to a Simpler, More Cooperative, Just and Ecologically Sustainable Society*, and Swedish systems ecologist Folke Gunther.

12. This apparent familiarity with permaculture can be misleading. For an in-depth understanding see David Holmgren, *Permaculture: Principles and Pathways beyond Sustainability* (Hepburn, Victoria, Australia: Holmgren Design Services, 2002). For an overview see 'The Essence of Permaculture' at www.holmgren.com.au ('Writings' page).

13. The 2007 *Living Planet Report* recently released by the Worldwide Fund for Nature claims that the only truly sustainable country in the world is Cuba – sustainable development being defined as a commitment to 'improving the quality of human life while living within the carrying capacity of supporting ecosystems'. The two key parameters employed by the WWF for measuring sustainable development were the United Nations Development Programme's (UNDP) Human Development Index (HDI) as the indicator of human well-being – calculated from life expectancy, literacy and education, and per capita GDP; and the Ecological Footprint, calculated at 1.8 global hectares per person, to measure the demand on the biosphere. Cuba was the ONLY country on Earth to achieve both criteria for sustainable development.

   In terms of ecological footprint, Australia rates as the sixth highest nation on Earth. If everyone lived like the average Australian we'd need almost four planets to support the Earth's current population.

14. This theme about permaculture as a change process is one that runs right through my *Permaculture: Principles and Pathways beyond Sustainability*.

Chapter 3

1. See the review of recent evidence by Carbon Equity, 'The Big Melt: Lessons from the Arctic Summer of 2007'," available on www.carbonequity.info.

2. See Richard Heinberg's 'Big Melt Meets Big Empty,' 2007, http://globalpublicmedia.com/richard_heinbergs_museletter_big_melt_meets_big_empty.

3. See Colin Campbell and Jean Laherrere, 'The End of Cheap Oil', *Scientific American* (March 1998). Reproduced at www.dieoff.org/page140.htm.

4. In late 2007 the IEA chief economist Fatih Birol gave a presentation that marked a major turning point in the official position of the IEA on future energy supplies. The presentation acknowledged peaking of oil production outside core OPEC countries and the likelihood that global demand will grow faster than supply. See this article at The Oil Drum: http://europe.theoildrum.com/node/3336#more.

5. See Chris Vernon, 'Coal: The Roundup', http://europe.theoildrum.com/node/2726/, which looks at five studies released in 2007 suggesting that there is less coal than previously thought, and the Energy Watch Group 2007 report (pdf).

6. By the International Energy Agency.

7. See the Energy Watch Group's Oil Report, 2007, www.energywatchgroup.de/Erdoel-Report.32+M5d637b1e38d.0.html.

8. Australia is one of the few long-affluent countries that might continue to 'prosper' based on nonrenewable resource extraction. These longer-term prospects do not detract from the potential of a short-term crisis, owing to Australia losing 20 to 30 per cent of its oil imports by 2012 from collapsing production and rapidly rising consumption in its main sources of supply in South-East Asia. See Aeldric, 'Australia and the Export Land Model', The Oil Drum, 2008, http://anz.theoildrum.com/node/3657#more.

9. See Ugo Bardi, 'Universal Mining Machines', The Oil Drum, 2008, http://europe.theoildrum.com/node/3451.

10. EROEI (Energy return on energy invested) is a measure of the degree to which any energy source (those with a EROEI above one) can sustain

the rest of society outside the energy-harvesting sector and so lead to the creation of real wealth.

11. See the Emergy Systems Website for a current explanation of these methods: www.emergysystems.org/.

12. See original article 'World Energy to 2050' at Paul Chefurka's website, www.paulchefurka.ca/WEAP2/WEAP2.html (also published at The Oil Drum, Canada, November 2007).

13. See Howard T. Odum, *Environmental Accounting: Emergy and Environmental Decision Making* (New York: Wiley, 1996).

14. See Jon Friese, The Oil Drum Website, www.theoildrum.com/node/3673#more.

15. See 'Peak Phosphorus', Energy Bulletin, www.energybulletin.net/33164.html.

16. www.richardheinberg.com/books.

17. See, for example, C. Hamilton, *Growth Fetish* (Sydney, Australia: Allen & Unwin, 2003).

18. Daniel Quinn gives the analogy of the loss of 200 species a day being equivalent to people who live in a tall brick building and every day knock 200 bricks out of the lower floor walls to continuously build new stories on the top. See *What A Way To Go: Life at the End of Empire* DVD 2007, a hard-hitting but inspiring overview of climate change, peak oil, population overshoot and species extinction, their cultural origins, and what sane responses remain open to us at this late stage.

Chapter 4

1. The well-credentialed Hirsch Report to the US government made these assessments assuming a collective societal effort similar to that mobilized in World War II. www.netl.doe.gov/publications/others/pdf/Oil_Peaking_NETL.pdf.

2. For example, see Lester Brown's work at www.earth-policy.org.

3. See Hopkins' *The Transition Handbook* for more on the rationale and methods for stimulating this change.

4. The key finding is that energy inequities between countries will increase.

5. It may be unrealistic to expect any open acknowledgment by governments and institutions of the severity of the challenges posed by these scenarios without a major crisis that breaks the paradigm of continuous economic growth.

6. The failure of global trade negotiations at Cancun, Mexico, in 2003 to lock in global trade agreements can now be seen as the last desperate effort to maintain the fruits of globalisation for the corporations before the onset of resource nationalism.

7. For example, Russia has being using the tight supply of gas and oil to enforce world prices on Eastern European countries and in the process giving warning to Western European countries about their vulnerabilities and dependence. Turning off the gas for even short periods has acted as a powerful enforcer. Similar actions by Argentina in cutting flows through new pipelines to Chile in response to shortages at home may force Chile to negotiate supplies from its old enemy Bolivia.

8. Also modelling by Stewart Staniford (Fermenting The Food Supply, on The Oil Drum website www.theoildrum.com/node/2431) suggests that steeply rising oil prices can accelerate demand for biofuels to consume unlimited proportions of world grain production within seven years, leading to global famine on a massive scale. Without regulation by government, free and global markets will see motorists in rich countries outbid the global poor for food.

9. The very large but unused detention facilities built for the US government by the Halliburton Corporation in several states of the United States raises questions about their likely use. www.prisonplanet.com/articles/february2006/010206detentioncamps.htm.

10. Superrationalism in this context recognises the energetic/ecological basis of human systems without any recognition of higher values or consciousness typified by spiritual and ethical frameworks that constrain the exercise of power.

11. In Australia, where a single large city dominates in each state, state government may be thought of as a bioregional government controlling a city and its economic hinterland.

12. For example, increases in medical intervention, legal litigation, and even crime and accidents all contribute to GDP.

13. An increasing number of peak-oil experts are suggesting the current peak of crude production in May 2005 may mark the beginning of a plateau that will end about 2010 in an accelerating decline.

14. For a review of the latest evidence of acceleration in climate change well beyond any previously credible predictions, see 'The Big Melt: Lessons from the Arctic Summer of 2007', available on www.carbonequity.info.

15. Triage is a process for managing the medical care of the injured during war or natural disasters where not all victims can be saved with the available resources. Those that have a chance of survival are the focus of

most attention while the others are given palliative care to ease their pain.

16. These are plants that grow better in foreign environments than in their original environment; usually called invasive species by conservationists. See 'Weeds or Wild Nature' at HDS website, www.holmgren.com.au/html/Writings/weeds.html.

17. Following the massive earthquake in 1960 around Valdivia in southern Chile, huge new wetlands were created following subsidence of the land. These wetlands had very high biological productivity based on an exotic aquatic plant that supported huge new populations of swans. The wetlands were recognised as being of global conservation significance under the RAMSAR convention. More recently, pollution from a local cellulose plant has led to a collapse in the population of swans.

Chapter 5

1. Helena Norbert-Hodge and Vandana Shiva are perhaps the most articulate critics of how these globalisation processes have adversely affected traditional communities in Ladakh and India, respectively.

2. Richard Heinberg, in *Powerdown: Options and Actions for a Post-Carbon World* (Gabriola Island, BC: New Society Publishers, 2004), provides an overview of some of the lessons from Cuba, Zimbabwe and North Korea. Dmitry Orlov has used his experience and study of the collapse of the Soviet Union as a model to understand the likely effects of peak oil on the United States. See 'Closing the Collapse Gap: The USSR Was Better Prepared for Collapse Than the US', Energy Bulletin, www.energybulletin.net/23259.html.

   The Power of Community: How Cuba Survived Peak Oil, a film by the Community Solution, has popularised the positive aspects of the Cuban case study. See the website www.powerofcommunity.org/cm/index.php.

3. For detailed documentation of the development of urban agriculture in Cuba see M. C. Cruz and R. S. Medina, *Agriculture in the City: A Key to Sustainability in Havana, Cuba* (Kingston, Jamaica: Ian Randle Publishers, 2003).

4. Personal communication, Roberto Perez, Cuban permaculturist featured in the documentary film *The Power of Community*.

5. I was not able to confirm this while in Cuba.

6. A shift to greater use of goats and less use of cattle would make Cuban agriculture more productive and sustainable.

7. Permaculture course-participant discussion at Gaia Ecovillage and personal communication, Pam Morgan, research in progress.

8. The projection of energy descent as an opportunity for economic and community renewal at the local level is illustrated by the rapidly growing Transition Towns movement in Britain, initiated by permaculture teacher Rob Hopkins. See Transition Culture website, http://transitionculture. org/ and the previously mentioned book by Hopkins, *The Transition Handbook*.

9. Clearly this is only likely if there also remains enough of a global economy to buy Australia's mineral and fossil-fuel wealth (and to generate the greenhouse-gas emissions that are fundamental to the brown-tech scenario).

10. Documents and statements of some American neoconservatives are almost open in acknowledging this future.

11. See Wikipedia for summary and links, http://en.wikipedia.org/wiki/ The_Natural_Step.

12. Rising energy costs will see fewer resources available for conservation projects that are not also productive of food, fodder and/or fuel. Changing climate will involve migration of plant and animal species on a scale that will overwhelm efforts to maintain and reinstate locally indigenous ecologies.

13. See 'Permaculture: Do We Need Principles?' in David Holmgren, *Collected Writings* vol. 2 (eBook), www.holmgren.com.au/html/ Publications/CollectedWritings.html.

Chapter 6

1. See http://en.wikipedia.org/wiki/William_Irwin_Thompson.

INDEX

THE TRANSITION HANDBOOK

From oil dependency to local resilience

Rob Hopkins

Founder of the Transition Network

"The Transition movement is the best news there's been for a long time, and this manual is a goldmine of inspiration to get you started."
Phil England, New Internationalist

We live in an oil-dependent world. Most people don't want to think about what will happen when the oil runs out, but *The Transition Handbook* shows how the profound and inevitable changes ahead can have a positive effect. They can lead to the rebirth of local communities, which will generate their own fuel, food and housing. They can unleash a local 'skilling-up', so that people have more control over their lives. *The Transition Handbook* is the manual that will guide communities to begin this 'energy descent' journey. The argument that 'small is inevitable' is upbeat and positive, as well as utterly convincing. Read this book!

ISBN 978 1 900322 18 8   £12.95 paperback

THE TRANSITION TIMELINE

For a local, resilient future

Shaun Chamberlin

"*The Transition Timeline* is a hugely valuable manual for anyone committed to turning dreams into reality. Don't just read this book – use it to change your world." Caroline Lucas, MEP

The Transition Timeline lightens the fear of our uncertain future, providing a map of what we are facing and the different pathways available to us. It describes possible scenarios over the next twenty years, ranging from Denial to the Transition Vision. The practical, realistic details of this Transition Vision are examined in depth, covering key areas such as food, energy, demographics, transport and healthcare.

ISBN 978 1 900322 56 0   £12.95 paperback